MznLnx

Missing Links Exam Preps

Exam Prep for

Modern Geometries

Smart, 5th Edition

The MznLnx Exam Prep is your link from the texbook and lecture to your exams.
The MznLnx Exam Preps are unauthorized and comprehensive reviews of your textbooks.

All material provided by MznLnx and Rico Publications (c) 2010
Textbook publishers and textbook authors do not particpate in or contribute to these reviews.

MznLnx

Rico
Publications

Exam Prep for Modern Geometries
5th Edition
Smart

Publisher: Raymond Houge
Assistant Editor: Michael Rouger
Text and Cover Designer: Lisa Buckner
Marketing Manager: Sara Swagger
Project Manager, Editorial Production: Jerry Emerson
Art Director: Vernon Lowerui

Product Manager: Dave Mason
Editorial Assitant: Rachel Guzmanji
Pedagogy: Debra Long
Cover Image: Jim Reed/Getty Images
Text and Cover Printer: City Printing, Inc.
Compositor: Media Mix, Inc.

(c) 2010 Rico Publications

ALL RIGHTS RESERVED. No part of this work covered by the copyright may be reproduced or used in any form or by an means--graphic, electronic, or mechanical, including photocopying, recording, taping, Web distribution, information storage, and retrieval systems, or in any other manner--without the written permission of the publisher.

Printed in the United States
ISBN:

For more information about our products, contact us at:
Dave.Mason@RicoPublications.com

For permission to use material from this text or product, submit a request online to:
Dave.Mason@RicoPublications.com

Contents

CHAPTER 1
Sets of Axioms and Finite Geometries — 1

CHAPTER 2
Geometric Transformations — 13

CHAPTER 3
Convexity — 27

CHAPTER 4
Modern Euclidean Geometry, Theory, and Applications — 37

CHAPTER 5
Constructions — 52

CHAPTER 6
The Transformation of Inversion — 58

CHAPTER 7
Projective Geometry — 63

CHAPTER 8
Geometric Introduction to Topological Transformations — 78

CHAPTER 9
Non-Euclidean Geometries — 87

ANSWER KEY — 109

TO THE STUDENT

COMPREHENSIVE

The *MznLnx* Exam Prep series is designed to help you pass your exams. Editors at MznLnx review your textbooks and then prepare these practice exams to help you master the textbook material. Unlike study guides, workbooks, and practice tests provided by the texbook publisher and textbook authors, *MznLnx* gives you **all** of the material in each chapter in exam form, not just samples, so you can be sure to nail your exam.

MECHANICAL

The MznLnx Exam Prep series creates exams that will help you learn the subject matter as well as test you on your understanding. Each question is designed to help you master the concept. Just working through the exams, you gain an understanding of the subject--its a simple mechanical process that produces success.

INTEGRATED STUDY GUIDE AND REVIEW

MznLnx is not just a set of exams designed to test you, its also a comprehensive review of the subject content. Each exam question is also a review of the concept, making sure that you will get the answer correct without having to go to other sources of material. You learn as you go! Its the easiest way to pass an exam.

HUMOR

Studying can be tedious and dry. MznLnx's instructional design includes moderate humor within the exam questions on occassion, to break the tedium and revitalize the brain

Chapter 1. Sets of Axioms and Finite Geometries

1. The _____ is an ancient Egyptian mathematical papyrus after its first owner, Egyptologist Vladimir GoleniÅ¡Ä ev. It later entered the collection of the Pushkin State Museum of Fine Arts in Moscow, where it remains today. Based on the palaeography of the hieratic text, it probably dates to the Eleventh dynasty of Egypt. Approximately 18 feet long and varying between 1 1/2 and 3 inches wide, its format was divided into 25 problems with solutions by the Soviet Orientalist Vasily Vasilievich Struve in 1930.

    a. Moscow Mathematical Papyrus
    b. 11-cell
    c. -module
    d. 1-center problem

2. A _____ is a building where the outer surfaces are triangular and converge at a point. The base of a _____ is usually trilateral or quadrilateral (but may be of any polygon shape), meaning that a _____ usually has four or five faces. A _____'s design, with the majority of the weight closer to the ground, means that less material higher up on the _____ will be pushing down from above: this allowed early civilizations to create stable monumental structures.

    a. 11-cell
    b. 1-center problem
    c. -module
    d. Pyramid

3. The _____ (also designated as: papyrus British Museum 10057, and pBM 10058), is named after Alexander Henry Rhind, a Scottish antiquarian, who purchased the papyrus in 1858 in Luxor, Egypt; it was apparently found during illegal excavations in or near the Ramesseum. It dates to around 1650 B.C. The British Museum, where the papyrus is now kept, acquired it in 1864 along with the Egyptian Mathematical Leather Roll, also owned by Henry Rhind; there are a few small fragments held by the Brooklyn Museum in New York. It is one of the two well-known Mathematical Papyri along with the Moscow Mathematical Papyrus.

    a. 11-cell
    b. -module
    c. 1-center problem
    d. Rhind Mathematical Papyrus

4. A _____ is a triangle in which one angle is a right angle.

The side opposite the right angle is called the hypotenuse (side [BC] in the figure below.) In addition, the sides adjacent to the right angle are called legs or catheti (singular: cathetus.)

    a. Simple polygon
    b. Stellation
    c. Right triangle
    d. Polygonal chain

Chapter 1. Sets of Axioms and Finite Geometries

5. A _____ is one of the basic shapes of geometry: a polygon with three corners or vertices and three sides or edges which are line segments. A _____ with vertices A, B, and C is denoted ABC.

In Euclidean geometry any three non-collinear points determine a unique _____ and a unique plane (i.e. a two-dimensional Euclidean space.)

   a. -module
   b. Brocard point
   c. 1-center problem
   d. Triangle

6. In mathematics, a _____ could be any function mapping a set X onto another set or onto itself. However, often the set X has some additional algebraic or geometric structure and the term '_____' refers to a function from X to itself which preserves this structure.

Examples include linear _____s and affine _____s such as rotations, reflections and translations.

   a. 1-center problem
   b. Transformation
   c. Codomain
   d. -module

7. In geometry and trigonometry, an _____ is the figure formed by two rays sharing a common endpoint, called the vertex of the _____ . The magnitude of the _____ is the 'amount of rotation' that separates the two rays, and can be measured by considering the length of circular arc swept out when one ray is rotated about the vertex to coincide with the other Where there is no possibility of confusion, the term '_____' is used interchangeably for both the geometric configuration itself and for its angular magnitude (which is simply a numerical quantity.)

   a. ADE classification
   b. AA postulate
   c. ADHM construction
   d. Angle

8. In the field of mathematical logic, a clear distinction is made between two notions of _____s: logical _____s and non-logical _____s (somewhat similar to the ancient distinction between '_____s' and 'postulates' respectively)

These are certain formulas in a formal language that are universally valid, that is, formulas that are satisfied by every assignment of values. Usually one takes as logical _____s at least some minimal set of tautologies that is sufficient for proving all tautologies in the language; in the case of predicate logic more logical _____s than that are required, in order to prove logical truths that are not tautologies in the strict sense.

Chapter 1. Sets of Axioms and Finite Geometries   3

In propositional logic it is common to take as logical _____s all formulae of the following forms, where φ, χ, and ψ can be any formulae of the language and where the included primitive connectives are only '¬' for negation of the immediately following proposition and '→' for implication from antecedent to consequent propositions:

1. $\phi \to (\psi \to \phi)$
2. $(\phi \to (\psi \to \chi)) \to ((\phi \to \psi) \to (\phi \to \chi))$
3. $(\neg\phi \to \neg\psi) \to (\psi \to \phi)$.

Each of these patterns is an _____ schema, a rule for generating an infinite number of _____s. For example, if A, B, and C are propositional variables, then $A \to (B \to A)$ and $(A \to \neg B) \to (C \to (A \to \neg B))$ are both instances of _____ schema 1, and hence are _____s.

a. AA postulate
b. ADE classification
c. Inductive reasoning
d. Axiom

9. _____ is the study and practice of making geographical maps. Combining science, aesthetics, and technique, _____ builds on the premise that reality can be modeled in ways that communicate spatial information effectively.

The fundamental problems of _____ are to:

- Set the map's agenda and select traits of the object to be mapped. This is the concern of map editing. Traits may be physical, such as roads or land masses, or may be abstract, such as toponyms or political boundaries.
- Represent the terrain of the mapped object on flat media. This is the concern of map projections.
- Eliminate characteristics of the mapped object that are not relevant to the map's purpose. This is the concern of generalization.
- Reduce the complexity of the characteristics that will be mapped. This is also the concern of generalization.
- Orchestrate the elements of the map to best convey its message to its audience. This is the concern of map design.

Copy (1475) of St. Isidore's TO map of the world.

The earliest known map is a matter of some debate, both because the definition of 'map' is not sharp and because some artifacts speculated to be maps might actually be something else. A wall painting, which may depict the ancient Anatolian city of >Çatalh>öy>ük (previously known as Catal Huyuk or >Çatal H>üy>ük), has been dated to the late 7th millennium BCE. Other known maps of the ancient world include the Minoan 'House of the Admiral' wall painting from c.

Chapter 1. Sets of Axioms and Finite Geometries

   a. 1-center problem
   b. 11-cell
   c. -module
   d. Cartography

10. In mathematics, a _____ section is a curve obtained by intersecting a cone (more precisely, a circular conical surface) with a plane. A _____ section is therefore a restriction of a quadric surface to the plane. The _____ sections were named and studied as long ago as 200 BC, when Apollonius of Perga undertook a systematic study of their properties.

   a. 1-center problem
   b. -module
   c. 11-cell
   d. Conic

11. _____ a branch of earth sciences, is the scientific discipline that deals with the measurement and representation of the Earth, including its gravitational field, in a three-dimensional time-varying space. Geodesists also study geodynamical phenomena such as crustal motion, tides, and polar motion. For this they design global and national control networks, using space and terrestrial techniques while relying on datums and coordinate systems.

   a. 1-center problem
   b. Geodesy
   c. -module
   d. 11-cell

12. A _____ is a visual representation of an area--a symbolic depiction highlighting relationships between elements of that space such as objects, regions, and themes.

Many _____s are static two-dimensional, geometrically accurate (or approximately accurate) representations of three-dimensional space, while others are dynamic or interactive, even three-dimensional. Although most commonly used to depict geography, _____s may represent any space, real or imagined, without regard to context or scale; e.g. Brain mapping, DNA mapping, and extraterrestrial mapping.

   a. 1-center problem
   b. -module
   c. Map
   d. 11-cell

Chapter 1. Sets of Axioms and Finite Geometries 5

13. The _____ is a cylindrical map projection presented by the Flemish geographer and cartographer Gerardus Mercator, in 1569. It became the standard map projection for nautical purposes because of its ability to represent lines of constant course, known as rhumb lines or loxodromes, as straight segments. While the linear scale is constant in all directions around any point, thus preserving the angles and the shapes of small objects (which makes the projection conformal), the _____ distorts the size and shape of large objects, as the scale increases from the Equator to the poles, where it becomes infinite.
   a. Stereographic projection
   b. Mercator projection
   c. 1-center problem
   d. -module

14. In mathematics, a _____ is a flat surface. _____s can arise as subspaces of some higher dimensional space, as with the walls of a room, or they may enjoy an independent existence in their own right, as in the setting of Euclidean geometry
   a. Parallelogram law
   b. Simple polytope
   c. Pendent
   d. Plane

15. In geometry, topology and related branches of mathematics a spatial _____ describes a specific object within a given space that consists of neither volume, area, length, nor any other higher dimensional analogue. Thus, a _____ is a 0-dimensional object. Because of their nature as one of the simplest geometric concepts, they are often used in one form or another as the fundamental constituents of geometry, physics, vector graphics, and many other fields.
   a. 1-center problem
   b. -module
   c. Bounded
   d. Point

16. In the field of mathematical logic, a clear distinction is made between two notions of axioms: _____ and non-_____

These are certain formulas in a formal language that are universally valid, that is, formulas that are satisfied by every assignment of values. Usually one takes as _____ at least some minimal set of tautologies that is sufficient for proving all tautologies in the language; in the case of predicate logic more _____ than that are required, in order to prove logical truths that are not tautologies in the strict sense.

In propositional logic it is common to take as _____ all formulae of the following forms, where φ, χ, and ψ can be any formulae of the language and where the included primitive connectives are only '¬' for negation of the immediately following proposition and '→' for implication from antecedent to consequent propositions:

1. $\phi \to (\psi \to \phi)$
2. $(\phi \to (\psi \to \chi)) \to ((\phi \to \psi) \to (\phi \to \chi))$
3. $(\neg\phi \to \neg\psi) \to (\psi \to \phi)$.

Each of these patterns is an axiom schema, a rule for generating an infinite number of axioms. For example, if A, B, and C are propositional variables, then $A \to (B \to A)$ and $(A \to \neg B) \to (C \to (A \to \neg B))$ are both instances of axiom schema 1, and hence are axioms.

a. Theorem
b. Logical axioms
c. Contrapositive
d. Logically equivalent

17. In formal mathematical logic, the concept of a _____ may be taken to mean a formula that can be derived according to the derivation rules of a fixed formal system. The statements of a theory as expressed in a formal language are called its elementary _____s and are said to be true.

The essential property of _____s is that they are derivable using a fixed set of inference rules and axioms without any additional assumptions.

a. Theorem
b. Logical axioms
c. Rule of inference
d. Proof

18. A _____ of a curve is the envelope of a family of congruent circles centered on the curve. It generalises the concept of _____ lines.

It is sometimes called the offset curve but the term 'offset' often refers also to translation.

a. Trisectrix of Maclaurin
b. Cissoid
c. Cassini oval
d. Parallel

19. In geometry, the _____ is a distinctive axiom in what is now called Euclidean geometry. It states that:

If a line segment intersects two straight lines forming two interior angles on the same side that sum to less than two right angles, then the two lines, if extended indefinitely, meet on that side on which the angles sum to less than two right angles.

Euclidean geometry is the study of geometry that satisfies all of Euclid's axioms, including the _____.

a. Parallel postulate
b. Hypotenuse
c. Confocal
d. Concyclic points

20. In mathematics, _____ geometry describes hyperbolic and elliptic geometry, which are contrasted with Euclidean geometry. The essential difference between Euclidean and _____ geometry is the nature of parallel lines. Euclid's fifth postulate, the parallel postulate, is equivalent to Playfair's postulate, which states that, within a two-dimensional plane, for any given line l and a point A, which is not on l, there is exactly one line through A that does not intersect l.
a. Codimension
b. Coplanar
c. Coaxial
d. Non-Euclidean

21. A non-Euclidean geometry is characterized by a non-vanishing Riemann curvature tensor. Examples of _____ include the hyperbolic and elliptic geometry, which are contrasted with a Euclidean geometry. The essential difference between Euclidean and non-Euclidean geometry is the nature of parallel lines.
a. Non-Euclidean geometries
b. -module
c. 11-cell
d. 1-center problem

Chapter 1. Sets of Axioms and Finite Geometries

22. In mathematics _____ is the study of geometric properties which are invariant under projective transformations. The field of _____ is itself divided into many subfields, two examples of which are projective algebraic geometry (the study of projective varieties) and projective differential geometry (the study of differential invariants of the projective transformations.)

_____, like affine and Euclidean geometry, can be developed from the Erlangen program of Felix Klein.

   a. John ellipsoid
   b. Geometric probability
   c. Birational geometry
   d. Projective geometry

23. In geometry, two sets of points are called _____ if one can be transformed into the other by an isometry, i.e., a combination of translations, rotations and reflections. Less formally, two figures are _____ if they have the same shape and size, but are in different positions (for instance one may be rotated, flipped, or simply placed somewhere else).
   a. Congruent
   b. -module
   c. Bounded
   d. 1-center problem

24. In geometry, _____ is the study of a type of transformations of the Euclidean plane, called inversions. These transformations preserve angles and map generalized circles into generalized circles, where a generalized circle means either a circle or a line (a circle with infinite radius.) Many difficult problems in geometry become much more tractable when an inversion is applied.
   a. AA postulate
   b. ADHM construction
   c. ADE classification
   d. Inversive geometry

25. _____ is a mathematical discipline that uses the methods of differential and integral calculus to study problems in geometry. The theory of plane and space curves and of surfaces in the three-dimensional Euclidean space formed the basis for its initial development in the eighteenth and nineteenth century. Since the late nineteenth century, _____ has grown into a field concerned more generally with geometric structures on differentiable manifolds.
   a. Darboux vector
   b. Nonmetricity tensor
   c. Chern-Weil theory
   d. Differential geometry

26. A _____ is generally 'a rough or fragmented geometric shape that can be split into parts, each of which is (at least approximately) a reduced-size copy of the whole,' a property called self-similarity. The term was coined by Beno>ît Mandelbrot in 1975 and was derived from the Latin fractus meaning 'broken' or 'fractured.' A mathematical _____ is based on an equation that undergoes iteration, a form of feedback based on recursion.

A _____ often has the following features:

- It has a fine structure at arbitrarily small scales.
- It is too irregular to be easily described in traditional Euclidean geometric language.
- It is self-similar .
- It has a Hausdorff dimension which is greater than its topological dimension (although this requirement is not met by space-filling curves such as the Hilbert curve.)
- It has a simple and recursive definition.

Because they appear similar at all levels of magnification, _____s are often considered to be infinitely complex (in informal terms.) Natural objects that approximate _____s to a degree include clouds, mountain ranges, lightning bolts, coastlines, and snow flakes.

a. -module
b. Julia set
c. Fractal
d. Disjunction

27. Problems of the following type, and their solution techniques, were first studied in the nineteenth century, and the general topic became known as _____.

- (Buffon's needle) What is the chance that a needle dropped randomly onto a floor marked with equally spaced parallel lines will cross one of the lines?

- What is the mean length of a random chord of a unit circle? (cf. Bertrand's paradox.)

- What is the chance that three random points in the plane form an acute (rather than obtuse) triangle?

- What is the mean area of the polygonal regions formed when randomly-oriented lines are spread over the plane?

For mathematical development see the concise monograph Solomon.

Since the late twentieth century the topic has split into two topics with different emphases.

a. Geometric probability
b. Coxeter group
c. Lateral surface
d. Lipschitz domain

28. In digital imaging, a _____ is the smallest item of information in an image. _____s are normally arranged in a 2-dimensional grid, and are often represented using dots, squares, or rectangles. Each _____ is a sample of an original image, where more samples typically provide more-accurate representations of the original.
   a. 1-center problem
   b. Raster graphics
   c. Pixel
   d. -module

29. A _____ or tiling of the plane is a collection of plane figures that fills the plane with no overlaps and no gaps. One may also speak of _____s of the parts of the plane or of other surfaces. Generalizations to higher dimensions are also possible.
   a. Tessellation
   b. Crystal system
   c. Screw axis
   d. Symmetry

30. The _____ is a professional society that focuses on mathematics accessible at the undergraduate level. Members include university, college, and high school teachers; graduate and undergraduate students; pure and applied mathematicians; computer scientists; statisticians; and many others in academia, government, business, and industry.

The MAA was founded in 1915 and is headquartered in Washington, D.C..

   a. -module
   b. Mathematical Association of America
   c. 11-cell
   d. 1-center problem

31. _____ is a form of argument in which a proposition is disproven by following its implications to a logical but absurd consequence.

An example of a _____ would be to note the consequences of an ad coelum theory of property would be that a land owner would have ownership over other planets.

Attempts at making a _____ argument can easily create a straw man fallacy if it distorts the proposition which one is trying to disprove.

a. 11-cell
b. 1-center problem
c. -module
d. Reductio ad absurdum

32. In geometry, the relations of _____ are those such as 'lies on' between points and lines (as in 'point P lies on line L'), and 'intersects' (as in 'line L_1 intersects line L_2', in three-dimensional space.) That is, they are the binary relations describing how subsets meet. The propositions of _____ stated in terms of them are statements such as 'any two lines in a plane meet'.

a. Incidence
b. ADHM construction
c. AA postulate
d. ADE classification

33. In category theory, a branch of mathematics, duality is a correspondence between properties of a category C and so-called _____ properties of the opposite category C^{op}. Given a statement regarding the category C, by interchanging the source and target of each morphism as well as interchanging the order of composing two morphisms, a corresponding _____ statement is obtained regarding the opposite category C^{op}. Duality, as such, is the assertion that truth is invariant under this operation on statements.

a. 11-cell
b. -module
c. Dual
d. 1-center problem

34. A _____ is any geometric system that has only a finite number of points. Euclidean geometry, for example, is not finite, because a Euclidean line contains infinitely many points, in fact precisely the same number of points as there are real numbers. A _____ can have any (finite) number of dimensions.

a. -module
b. 11-cell
c. 1-center problem
d. Finite geometry

Chapter 1. Sets of Axioms and Finite Geometries

35. In geometry, the terms _____ and polar are used to describe a point and a line that have a unique reciprocal relationship with respect to a given conic section. If the point lies on the conic section, its polar is the tangent line to the conic section at that point.

For a given circle, the operation of reciprocation in a circle corresponds to transforming each point in the plane into its polar line and each line in the plane into its _____.

a. 11-cell
b. -module
c. Pole
d. 1-center problem

36. There are many distinct but interrelated dualities in which geometric or topological objects correspond to other objects of the same type, but with a reversal of the dimensions of the features of the objects. A classical example of this is the duality of the platonic solids, in which the cube and the octahedron form a dual pair, the dodecahedron and the icosahedron form a dual pair, and the tetrahedron is _____. The dual polyhedron of any of these polyhedra may be formed as the convex hull of the center points of each face of the primal polyhedron, so the vertices of the dual correspond one-for-one with the faces of the primal.

a. -module
b. 1-center problem
c. Self-dual
d. 11-cell

Chapter 2. Geometric Transformations

1. In mathematics, a _____ could be any function mapping a set X onto another set or onto itself. However, often the set X has some additional algebraic or geometric structure and the term '_____' refers to a function from X to itself which preserves this structure.

Examples include linear _____s and affine _____s such as rotations, reflections and translations.

   a. 1-center problem
   b. -module
   c. Codomain
   d. Transformation

2. In mathematics, the _____ of a function is the set Y into which all of the output of the function is constrained to fall. It is the set Y in the notation f: X >→ Y.

The _____ is part of the modern definition of a function f as a triple (X, Y, F), with F a subset of the Cartesian product X >× Y. The set of all elements of the form f(x), where x ranges over the elements of the domain X, is called the image of f. In general, the image of a function is a subset of its _____ but not necessarily the same set; a function that is not surjective has elements y in its _____ for which the equation f(x) = y does not have a solution.

   a. 1-center problem
   b. Transformation
   c. -module
   d. Codomain

3. _____ is the study and practice of making geographical maps. Combining science, aesthetics, and technique, _____ builds on the premise that reality can be modeled in ways that communicate spatial information effectively.

The fundamental problems of _____ are to:

   - Set the map's agenda and select traits of the object to be mapped. This is the concern of map editing. Traits may be physical, such as roads or land masses, or may be abstract, such as toponyms or political boundaries.
   - Represent the terrain of the mapped object on flat media. This is the concern of map projections.
   - Eliminate characteristics of the mapped object that are not relevant to the map's purpose. This is the concern of generalization.
   - Reduce the complexity of the characteristics that will be mapped. This is also the concern of generalization.
   - Orchestrate the elements of the map to best convey its message to its audience. This is the concern of map design.

Copy (1475) of St. Isidore's TO map of the world.

Chapter 2. Geometric Transformations

The earliest known map is a matter of some debate, both because the definition of 'map' is not sharp and because some artifacts speculated to be maps might actually be something else. A wall painting, which may depict the ancient Anatolian city of >Çatalh>öy>ük (previously known as Catal Huyuk or >Çatal H>üy>ük), has been dated to the late 7th millennium BCE. Other known maps of the ancient world include the Minoan 'House of the Admiral' wall painting from c.

a. 1-center problem
b. 11-cell
c. -module
d. Cartography

4. An _____ is a type of quadric surface that is a higher dimensional analogue of an ellipse. The equation of a standard axis-aligned _____ body in an xyz-Cartesian coordinate system is

where a and b are the equatorial radii (along the x and y axes) and c is the polar radius (along the z-axis), all of which are fixed positive real numbers determining the shape of the _____.

More generally, a not-necessarily-axis-aligned _____ is defined by the equation

where A is a symmetric positive definite matrix and x is a vector.

a. ADHM construction
b. Ellipsoid
c. AA postulate
d. ADE classification

5. In algebra and geometry, a _____ is a way of describing symmetries of objects using groups. The essential elements of the object are described by a set and the symmetries of the object are described by the symmetry group of this set, which consists of bijective transformations of the set. In this case, the group is also called a permutation group (especially if the set is finite or not a vector space) or transformation group (especially if the set is a vector space and the group acts like linear transformations of the set.)

Chapter 2. Geometric Transformations

a. 11-cell
b. 1-center problem
c. -module
d. Group action

6. In mathematics, associativity is a property that a binary operation can have. It means that, within an expression containing two or more of the same _____ operators in a row, the order that the operations are performed does not matter as long as the sequence of the operands is not changed. That is, rearranging the parentheses in such an expression will not change its value.
   a. Algebraic number
   b. Associativity
   c. Associative
   d. AA postulate

7. In mathematics, _____ is a property that a binary operation can have. It means that, within an expression containing two or more of the same associative operators in a row, the order that the operations are performed does not matter as long as the sequence of the operands is not changed. That is, rearranging the parentheses in such an expression will not change its value.
   a. Algebraic number
   b. AA postulate
   c. Associative
   d. Associativity

8. In mathematics, the _____ of a subset S in a topological space consists of all points which are intuitively 'close to S'. A point which is in the _____ of S is a point of _____ of S. The notion of _____ is in many ways dual to the notion of interior.

For S a subset of a Euclidean space, x is a point of _____ of S if every open ball centered at x contains a point of S (this point may be x itself).

This definition generalises to any subset S of a metric space X. Fully expressed, for X a metric space with metric d, x is a point of _____ of S if for every r > 0, there is a y in S such that the distance $d(x, y) < r$. (Again, we may have x = y.) Another way to express this is to say that x is a point of _____ of S if the distance $d(x, S) := \inf\{d(x, s) : s \in S\} = 0$.

Chapter 2. Geometric Transformations

a. 1-center problem
b. Bounded
c. Closure
d. -module

9. 3. A binary function f:A>×A >→ B is said to be _____ if:

>

The first known use of the term was in a French Journal published in 1814

Records of the implicit use of the _____ property go back to ancient times. The Egyptians used the _____ property of multiplication to simplify computing products.

a. 1-center problem
b. -module
c. Linear map
d. Commutative

10. An _____ is a group in which the result of applying the group operation to two group elements does not depend on their order _____ s generalize the arithmetic of addition of integers. They are named after Niels Henrik Abel.
a. ADE classification
b. AA postulate
c. Abelian group
d. ADHM construction

11. In geometry, an _____ polygon is a polygon which has all sides of the same length.

For instance, an _____ triangle is a triangle of equal edge lengths. All _____ triangles are similar to each other, and have 60 degree internal angles.

a. Octagon
b. Octadecagon
c. Enneagram
d. Equilateral

Chapter 2. Geometric Transformations

12. In geometry, an _____ is a triangle in which all three sides are equal. In traditional or Euclidean geometry, _____s are also equiangular; that is, all three internal angles are also congruent to each other and are each 60°. They are regular polygons, and can therefore also be referred to as regular triangles.

    a. Orthocenter
    b. ADE classification
    c. Equilateral triangle
    d. AA postulate

13. A _____ is one of the basic shapes of geometry: a polygon with three corners or vertices and three sides or edges which are line segments. A _____ with vertices A, B, and C is denoted ABC.

    In Euclidean geometry any three non-collinear points determine a unique _____ and a unique plane (i.e. a two-dimensional Euclidean space.)

    a. 1-center problem
    b. -module
    c. Brocard point
    d. Triangle

14. In mathematics, a _____ is the group of symmetries of a regular polygon, including both rotations and reflections. _____s are among the simplest examples of finite groups, and they play an important role in group theory, geometry, and chemistry.

    There are two competing notations for the _____ associated to a polygon with n sides. In geometry the group is denoted D_n, while in algebra the same group is denoted by D_{2n} to indicate the number of elements.

    a. Kurosh subgroup theorem
    b. Longest element of a Coxeter group
    c. Stallings' theorem about ends of groups
    d. Dihedral group

15. In mathematics, an _____, isometric isomorphism or congruence mapping is a distance-preserving isomorphism between metric spaces. Geometric figures which can be related by an _____ are called congruent.

    They are often used in constructions where one space is embedded in another space. For instance, the completion of a metric space M involves an _____ from M into M', a quotient set of the space of Cauchy sequences on M. The original space M is thus isometrically isomorphic to a subspace of a complete metric space, and it is usually identified with this subspace.

a. AA postulate
b. One-to-one
c. Isometry
d. Identity function

16. In mathematics, a _____ is a flat surface. _____s can arise as subspaces of some higher dimensional space, as with the walls of a room, or they may enjoy an independent existence in their own right, as in the setting of Euclidean geometry
   a. Simple polytope
   b. Parallelogram law
   c. Plane
   d. Pendent

17. In geometry, two sets of points are called _____ if one can be transformed into the other by an isometry, i.e., a combination of translations, rotations and reflections. Less formally, two figures are _____ if they have the same shape and size, but are in different positions (for instance one may be rotated, flipped, or simply placed somewhere else).
   a. Bounded
   b. 1-center problem
   c. -module
   d. Congruent

18. In Euclidean geometry, a _____ is moving every point a constant distance in a specified direction. It is one of the rigid motions (other rigid motions include rotation and reflection.) A _____ can also be interpreted as the addition of a constant vector to every point, or as shifting the origin of the coordinate system.
   a. Point reflection
   b. Reflection
   c. Rotation of axes
   d. Translation

19. A _____ is a movement of an object in a circular motion. A two-dimensional object rotates around a center (or point) of _____. A three-dimensional object rotates around a line called an axis.
   a. Rotation
   b. Similarity
   c. Square lattice
   d. Curve of constant width

Chapter 2. Geometric Transformations

20. In mathematics, a _____ is a map that transforms an object into its mirror image. For example, a _____ of the small English letter p in respect to a vertical line would look like q. In order to reflect a planar figure one needs the 'mirror' to be a line , while for _____s in the three-dimensional space one would use a plane for a mirror.
    a. Point reflection
    b. Translation
    c. Reflection
    d. Rotation of axes

21. In geometry, a _____ is a type of isometry of the Euclidean plane: the combination of a reflection in a line and a translation along that line. Reversing the order of combining gives the same result. Depending on context, we may consider a reflection a special case, where the translation vector is the zero vector.
    a. Point reflection
    b. Rotation of axes
    c. Glide reflection
    d. Translation

22. In chemistry, the _____ molecular geometry describes the arrangement of three or more atoms placed at an expected bond angle of 180°. _____ organic molecules, e.g. acetylene, are often described by invoking sp orbital hybridization for the carbon centers. Many _____ molecules exist, prominent examples include CO_2, HCN, and xenon difluoride.
    a. 11-cell
    b. Linear
    c. -module
    d. 1-center problem

23. In mathematics, a _____ is a function between two vector spaces that preserves the operations of vector addition and scalar multiplication. The expression 'linear operator' is in especially common use, for _____s from a vector space to itself In advanced mathematics, the definition of linear function coincides with the definition of _____.
    a. -module
    b. Linear map
    c. 11-cell
    d. 1-center problem

24. _____ is the mathematical operation of scaling one number by another. It is one of the four basic operations in elementary arithmetic (the others being addition, subtraction and division.)

_____ is defined for whole numbers in terms of repeated addition; for example, 3 multiplied by 4 (often said as '3 times 4') can be calculated by adding 3 copies of 4 together:

_____ of rational numbers (fractions) and real numbers is defined by systematic generalization of this basic idea.

a. 11-cell
b. -module
c. 1-center problem
d. Multiplication

25. In group theory, a _____ is a group that can be generated by a single element, in the sense that the group has an element g (called a 'generator' of the group) such that, when written multiplicatively, every element of the group is a power of g (a multiple of g when the notation is additive.) The 6th complex roots of unity form a _____ under multiplication. z is a primitive element, but z^2 is not, because the odd powers of z are not a power of z^2.

A group G is called cyclic if there exists an element g in G such that G = <g> = { g^n | n is an integer }.

a. -module
b. 11-cell
c. Cyclic group
d. 1-center problem

26. In formal mathematical logic, the concept of a _____ may be taken to mean a formula that can be derived according to the derivation rules of a fixed formal system. The statements of a theory as expressed in a formal language are called its elementary _____s and are said to be true.

The essential property of _____s is that they are derivable using a fixed set of inference rules and axioms without any additional assumptions.

a. Logical axioms
b. Proof
c. Rule of inference
d. Theorem

27. In mathematical analysis, an analytical proof is a proof of a theorem in analysis that only makes use of methods from analysis, and which does not make use of results from geometry. The term was first used by Bernard Bolzano, who first provided a non-_____ of his intermediate value theorem and then, several years later provided proof of the theorem which was free from intuitions concerning lines crossing each other at a point and so he felt happy calling analytic (Bolzano 1817.)

Bolzano's philosophical work encouraged a more abstract reading of when a demonstration could be regarded as analytic, where a proof is analytic if it does not go beyond its subject matter (Sebastik 2007.)

a. AA postulate
b. Analytic proof
c. ADE classification
d. ADHM construction

28. In mathematics, a _____ is a convincing demonstration (within the accepted standards of the field) that some mathematical statement is necessarily true. _____s are obtained from deductive reasoning, rather than from inductive or empirical arguments. That is, a _____ must demonstrate that a statement is true in all cases, without a single exception.

a. Theorem
b. Proof
c. Contrapositive
d. Logical axioms

29. In geometry, a polygon can be either _____ or concave.

A _____ polygon is a simple polygon whose interior is a _____ set. The following properties of a simple polygon are all equivalent to convexity:

- Every internal angle is less than 180 degrees.
- Every line segment between two vertices remains inside or on the boundary of the polygon.

A simple polygon is strictly _____ if every internal angle is strictly less than 180 degrees. Equivalently, a polygon is strictly _____ if every line segment between two nonadjacent vertices of the polygon is strictly interior to the polygon except at its endpoints.

a. Supporting hyperplane
b. Separating axis theorem
c. Convex combination
d. Convex

Chapter 2. Geometric Transformations

30. A _____ is an expression which compares quantities relative to each other. The most common examples involve two quantities, but in theory any number of quantities can be compared. In mathematical terms, they are represented by separating each quantity with a colon, for example the _____ 2:3, which is read as the _____ 'two to three'.
   a. Ratio
   b. -module
   c. Slope of a line
   d. Slope

31. One of the meanings of the terms _____ and _____ transformation (also called dilation) of a Euclidean space is a function f from the space into itself that multiplies all distances by the same positive scalar r, so that for any two points x and y we have

$$d(f(x), f(y)) = rd(x,y),$$

where 'd(x,y)' is the Euclidean distance from x to y. Two sets are called similar if one is the image of the other under such a _____.

A special case is a homothetic transformation or central _____: it neither involves rotation nor taking the mirror image.

   a. Square lattice
   b. Flat
   c. Similar
   d. Similarity

32. _____ is one of the basic operations in mathematical morphology. Originally developed for binary images, it has been expanded first to grayscale images, and then to complete lattices. The _____ operation usually uses a structuring element for probing and expanding the shapes contained in the input image.
   a. -module
   b. Dilation
   c. 11-cell
   d. 1-center problem

33. In mathematics, a _____ is a transformation of space which takes each line into a parallel line (in essence, a similarity that is similarly arranged). All dilatations form a group in either affine or Euclidean geometry. Typical examples of dilatations are translations, half-turns, and the identity transformation.

In Euclidean geometry, when not a translation, there is a unique number c by which distances in the dilatation are multiplied. It is called the ratio of magnification or dilation factor or similitude ratio. Such a transformation can be called an enlargement. More generally c can be negative; in that case it not only multiplies all distances by | c |, but also inverts all points with respect to the fixed point.

   a. Homothety
   b. Convex body
   c. Loomis-Whitney inequality
   d. Lateral surface

34. A _____ is a simple shape of Euclidean geometry consisting of those points in a plane which are the same distance from a given point called the centre. The common distance of the points of a _____ from its center is called its radius.

_____s are simple closed curves which divide the plane into two regions, an interior and an exterior.

   a. Circumcircle
   b. Gergonne point
   c. Circumscribed circle
   d. Circle

35. _____ is the boundless, three-dimensional extent in which objects and events occur and have relative position and direction. Physical _____ is often conceived in three linear dimensions, although modern physicists usually consider it, with time, to be part of the boundless four-dimensional continuum known as spacetime. In mathematics _____s with different numbers of dimensions and with different underlying structures can be examined.
   a. -module
   b. 1-center problem
   c. 11-cell
   d. Space

36. A _____ is generally 'a rough or fragmented geometric shape that can be split into parts, each of which is (at least approximately) a reduced-size copy of the whole,' a property called self-similarity. The term was coined by Beno>ît Mandelbrot in 1975 and was derived from the Latin fractus meaning 'broken' or 'fractured.' A mathematical _____ is based on an equation that undergoes iteration, a form of feedback based on recursion.

A _____ often has the following features:

- It has a fine structure at arbitrarily small scales.
- It is too irregular to be easily described in traditional Euclidean geometric language.
- It is self-similar .
- It has a Hausdorff dimension which is greater than its topological dimension (although this requirement is not met by space-filling curves such as the Hilbert curve.)
- It has a simple and recursive definition.

Because they appear similar at all levels of magnification, _____s are often considered to be infinitely complex (in informal terms.) Natural objects that approximate _____s to a degree include clouds, mountain ranges, lightning bolts, coastlines, and snow flakes.

a. -module
b. Disjunction
c. Julia set
d. Fractal

37. In mathematics, the _____ of a vector space V is the cardinality (i.e. the number of vectors) of a basis of V. It is sometimes called Hamel _____ or algebraic _____ to distinguish it from other types of _____. All bases of a vector space have equal cardinality and so the _____ of a vector space is uniquely defined. The _____ of the vector space V over the field F can be written as $\dim_F(V)$ or as [V : F], read '_____ of V over F'.

a. 11-cell
b. -module
c. 1-center problem
d. Dimension

38. The Koch snowflake (or Koch star) is a mathematical curve and one of the earliest fractal curves to have been described. It appeared in a 1904 paper titled 'On a continuous curve without tangents, constructible from elementary geometry' by the Swedish mathematician Helge von Koch. The _____ is a special case of the Césaro curve where $a = \frac{1}{2} + \frac{i}{\sqrt{12}}$, which is in turn a special case of the de Rham curve.

a. Koch snowflake
b. Gosper curve
c. Hilbert curve
d. Koch curve

39. _____ are a class of computational algorithms that rely on repeated random sampling to compute their results. _____ are often used when simulating physical and mathematical systems. Because of their reliance on repeated computation and random or pseudo-random numbers, _____ are most suited to calculation by a computer.

   a. 11-cell
   b. -module
   c. Monte Carlo methods
   d. 1-center problem

40. In mathematics, a _____ consists of the points through which a continuously moving point passes. This notion captures the intuitive idea of a geometrical one-dimensional object, which furthermore is connected in the sense of having no discontinuities or gaps. Simple examples include the sine wave as the basic _____ underlying simple harmonic motion, and the parabola.

   a. Dual curve
   b. Sectrix of Maclaurin
   c. Singular point
   d. Curve

41. The _____ is a plane fractal first described by Wacław Sierpiński in 1916. The carpet is a generalization of the Cantor set to two dimensions (another is Cantor dust.) Sierpiński demonstrated that this fractal is a universal curve, in that any possible one-dimensional graph, projected onto the two-dimensional plane, is homeomorphic to a subset of the _____.

   a. Multifractal system
   b. Fractal generating software
   c. Sierpinski carpet
   d. Cantor function

42. The _____ is a fractal named after the Polish mathematician Wacław Sierpiński who described it in 1915.

Originally constructed as a curve, this is one of the basic examples of self-similar sets, i.e. it is a mathematically generated pattern that can be reproducible at any magnification or reduction.

Comparing the _____ or the Sierpinski carpet to equivalent repetitive tiling arrangements, it is evident that similar structures can be built into any rep-tile arrangements.

   a. -module
   b. Sierpinski triangle
   c. 1-center problem
   d. 11-cell

Chapter 2. Geometric Transformations

43. In mathematics, the _____, introduced by German mathematician Georg Cantor in 1883, is a set of points lying on a single line segment that has a number of remarkable and deep properties. Through consideration of it, Cantor and others helped lay the foundations of modern general topology. Although Cantor himself defined the set in a general, abstract way, the most common modern construction is the Cantor ternary set, built by removing the middle thirds of a line segment.
   a. Ham sandwich theorem
   b. 1-center problem
   c. -module
   d. Cantor set

44. In mathematical analysis and related areas of mathematics, a set is called _____, if it is, in a certain sense, of finite size. Conversely a set which is not _____ is called unbounded.

A set S of real numbers is called _____ from above if there is a real number k such that k >≥ s for all s in S. The number k is called an upper bound of S. The terms _____ from below and lower bound are similarly defined.

   a. 11-cell
   b. -module
   c. Bounded
   d. 1-center problem

45. In mathematics, the _____, named after Benoît Mandelbrot, is a set of points in the complex plane, the boundary of which forms a fractal. Mathematically, the _____ can be defined as the set of complex values of c for which the orbit of 0 under iteration of the complex quadratic polynomial $z_{n+1} = z_n^2 + c$ remains bounded. That is, a complex number, c, is in the _____ if, when starting with $z_0=0$ and applying the iteration repeatedly, the absolute value of z_n never exceeds a certain number (that number depends on c) however large n gets.
   a. Hausdorff measure
   b. Lyapunov fractal
   c. Gravity set
   d. Mandelbrot set

Chapter 3. Convexity

1. In geometry, a polygon can be either _____ or concave.

A _____ polygon is a simple polygon whose interior is a _____ set. The following properties of a simple polygon are all equivalent to convexity:

- Every internal angle is less than 180 degrees.
- Every line segment between two vertices remains inside or on the boundary of the polygon.

A simple polygon is strictly _____ if every internal angle is strictly less than 180 degrees. Equivalently, a polygon is strictly _____ if every line segment between two nonadjacent vertices of the polygon is strictly interior to the polygon except at its endpoints.

a. Separating axis theorem
b. Convex combination
c. Convex
d. Supporting hyperplane

2. In mathematical analysis and related areas of mathematics, a set is called _____, if it is, in a certain sense, of finite size. Conversely a set which is not _____ is called unbounded.

A set S of real numbers is called _____ from above if there is a real number k such that k >≥ s for all s in S. The number k is called an upper bound of S. The terms _____ from below and lower bound are similarly defined.

a. 11-cell
b. 1-center problem
c. Bounded
d. -module

3. A curve <x> is said to be closed or a loop if <x> and if <x>. A _____ is thus a continuous mapping of the circle S^1; a simple _____ is also called a Jordan curve or a Jordan arc. The Jordan curve theorem states that such curves divide the plane into an 'interior' and an 'exterior'.
a. -module
b. Closed curve
c. 11-cell
d. 1-center problem

4. In mathematics, a _____ is a flat surface. _____s can arise as subspaces of some higher dimensional space, as with the walls of a room, or they may enjoy an independent existence in their own right, as in the setting of Euclidean geometry

a. Simple polytope
b. Pendent
c. Plane
d. Parallelogram law

5. In mathematics, a _____ is a curve in a Euclidian plane (cf. space curve.) The most frequently studied cases are smooth _____s (including piecewise smooth _____s), and algebraic _____s.
   a. Plane curve
   b. Heilbronn triangle problem
   c. Chirality
   d. Point group in two dimensions

6. In mathematics, a _____ consists of the points through which a continuously moving point passes. This notion captures the intuitive idea of a geometrical one-dimensional object, which furthermore is connected in the sense of having no discontinuities or gaps. Simple examples include the sine wave as the basic _____ underlying simple harmonic motion, and the parabola.
   a. Dual curve
   b. Singular point
   c. Sectrix of Maclaurin
   d. Curve

7. In mathematics, the _____ of a set S consists of all points of S that are intuitively 'not on the edge of S'. A point that is in the _____ of S is an _____ point of S.

The exterior of a set is the _____ of its complement; it consists of the points that are not in the set or its boundary.

The notion of the _____ of a set is a topological concept; it is not defined for all sets, but it is defined for sets that are a subset of a topological space.

   a. Interior
   b. ADHM construction
   c. ADE classification
   d. AA postulate

Chapter 3. Convexity

8. In geometry, topology and related branches of mathematics a spatial _____ describes a specific object within a given space that consists of neither volume, area, length, nor any other higher dimensional analogue. Thus, a _____ is a 0-dimensional object. Because of their nature as one of the simplest geometric concepts, they are often used in one form or another as the fundamental constituents of geometry, physics, vector graphics, and many other fields.
   a. Point
   b. 1-center problem
   c. Bounded
   d. -module

9. In topology and mathematics in general, the boundary of a subset S of a topological space X is the set of points which can be approached both from S and from the outside of S. More precisely, it is the set of points in the closure of S, not belonging to the interior of S. An element of the boundary of S is called a _____ of S. S is boundaryless when it contains no boundary, which is to say no _____ Notations used for boundary of a set S include bd(S), fr(S), and $>\partial$S. Some authors (for example Willard, in General Topology) use the term frontier, instead of boundary in an attempt to avoid confusion with the concept of boundary used in algebraic topology and manifold theory.

A connected component of the boundary of S is called a boundary component of S.

There are several common (and equivalent) definitions to the boundary of a subset S of a topological space X:

- the closure of S without the interior of S: $>\partial$S = >S S°.
- the intersection of the closure of S with the closure of its complement: $>\partial$S = >S >∩ >(X S).
- the set of points p of X such that every neighborhood of p contains at least one point of S and at least one point not of S.

Boundary of hyperbolic components of Mandelbrot set

Consider the real line R with the usual topology (i.e. the topology whose basis sets are open intervals.) One has

- $>\partial$(0,5) = $>\partial$[0,5) = $>\partial$(0,5] = $>\partial$[0,5] = {0,5}
- $>\partial$>∅ = >∅
- $>\partial$Q = R
- $>\partial$(Q >∩ [0,1]) = [0,1]

These last two examples illustrate the fact that the boundary of a dense set with empty interior is its closure.

In the space of rational numbers with the usual topology (the subspace topology of R), the boundary of >, where a is irrational, is empty.

a. Connected set
b. -module
c. 1-center problem
d. Boundary point

10. In mathematics, a topological space is called _____ if each of its open covers has a finite subcover. Otherwise it is called non-_____.

The Heine-Borel theorem shows that this definition is equivalent to 'closed and bounded' for subsets of Euclidean space. So a subset of Euclidean space R^n is called _____ if it is closed and bounded. For example, in R, the closed unit interval [0, 1] is _____, but the set of integers Z is not (it is not bounded) and neither is the half-open interval [0, 1) (it is not closed).

a. 1-center problem
b. Compact
c. 11-cell
d. -module

11. In vernacular terms, this states 'If P then Q', or, 'If Socrates is a man then Socrates is human.' In a conditional such as this, P is called the antecedent and Q the consequent. One statement is the _____ of the other just when its antecedent is the negated consequent of the other, and vice-versa. The _____ of the given example statement would be:

$$(\neg Q \to \neg P)$$

That is, 'If not-Q then not-P', or more clearly, 'If Q is not the case, then P is not the case.' Using our example, this is rendered 'If Socrates is not human, then Socrates is not a man.' This statement is said to be contraposed to the original, and is logically equivalent to it.

a. Theorem
b. Contrapositive
c. Logically equivalent
d. Logical axioms

12. In linear algebra, a (linear) _____ is a subset of a vector space that is closed under multiplication by positive scalars. In other words, a subset C of a real vector space V is a _____ if and only if >λx belongs to C for any x in C and any positive scalar >λ of V (or, more succinctly, if and only if >λC = C for any positive scalar >λ.)

A _____ is said to be pointed if it includes the null vector (origin) 0; otherwise it is said to be blunt.

Chapter 3. Convexity

a. Prismatic surface
b. Centerpoint
c. Complex line
d. Cone

13. In geometry, the _____ line (or simply the _____) to a curve at a given point is the straight line that 'just touches' the curve at that point (in the sense explained more precisely below.) As it passes through the point of tangency, the _____ line is 'going in the same direction' as the curve, and in this sense it is the best straight-line approximation to the curve at that point. The same definition applies to space curves and curves in n-dimensional Euclidean space.

a. Cartan connection
b. Metric signature
c. Measuring function
d. Tangent

14. In geometry, the _____ is a generalization of the notion of the tangent space to a manifold to the case of certain spaces with singularities.

Let K be a closed convex subset of a real vector space V and >∂K be the boundary of K. The solid _____ to K at a point x >∈ >∂K is the closure of the cone formed by all half-lines (or rays) emanating from x and intersecting K in at least one point y distinct from x. It is a convex cone in V and can also be defined as the intersection of the closed half-spaces of V containing K and bounded by the supporting hyperplanes of K at x.

a. Tangent cone
b. Cantitruncated alternated cubic honeycomb
c. Cantellated cubic honeycomb
d. Grothendieck connection

15. In mathematics, a _____ in n-dimensional Euclidean space R^n is a compact convex set with non-empty interior.

A _____ K is called symmetric if it is centrally symmetric with respect to the origin, i.e. a point x lies in K if and only if its antipode, >−x, also lies in K. Symmetric convex bodies are in a one-to-one correspondence with the unit balls of norms on R^n.

Important examples of convex bodies are the Euclidean ball, the hypercube and the cross-polytope.

a. Peaucellier-Lipkin linkage
b. Brascamp-Lieb inequality
c. Circumference
d. Convex body

16. A _____ is a path that surrounds an area. The word comes from the Greek peri and meter (measure.) The term may be used either for the path or its length.
a. Transversal line
b. Multilateration
c. Complementary angles
d. Perimeter

17. In chemistry, the _____ molecular geometry describes the arrangement of three or more atoms placed at an expected bond angle of 180°. _____ organic molecules, e.g. acetylene, are often described by invoking sp orbital hybridization for the carbon centers. Many _____ molecules exist, prominent examples include CO_2, HCN, and xenon difluoride.
a. -module
b. 11-cell
c. 1-center problem
d. Linear

18. In mathematics, _____ is a technique for optimization of a linear objective function, subject to linear equality and linear inequality constraints. Informally, _____ determines the way to achieve the best outcome (such as maximum profit or lowest cost) in a given mathematical model and given some list of requirements represented as linear equations.

More formally, given a polytope (for example, a polygon or a polyhedron), and a real-valued affine function

defined on this polytope, a _____ method will find a point in the polytope where this function has the smallest (or largest) value.

a. -module
b. 1-center problem
c. 11-cell
d. Linear programming

Chapter 3. Convexity

19. In technical applications of 3D computer graphics (CAx) such as computer-aided design and computer-aided manufacturing, _____s are one way of representing objects. The other ways are wireframe (lines and curves) and solids. Point clouds are also sometimes used as temporary ways to represent an object, with the goal of using the points to create one or more of the three permanent representations.
    a. Space partitioning
    b. Geometric primitive
    c. Solid modeling
    d. Surface

20. In mathematics a _____ is a closed manifold of dimension two, with a single connected component. Examples are spaces like the sphere, the torus, and the Klein bottle. They are classified by the genus and their orientability.
    a. Hyperbolic n-manifold
    b. Spinor bundle
    c. Circle-valued Morse theory
    d. Closed Surface

21. In mathematics, the _____ or convex envelope for a set of points X in a real vector space V is the minimal convex set containing X.

In computational geometry, it is common to use the term '_____' for the boundary of the minimal convex set containing a given non-empty finite set of points in the plane. Unless the points are collinear, the _____ in this sense is a simple closed polygonal chain.

    a. Convex combination
    b. Convex hull
    c. Separating axis theorem
    d. Geodesic convexity

22. A Reuleaux polygon is a curve of constant width - that is, a curve such that, if two parallel lines are drawn tangent to the curve in any orientation, the distance between them is fixed. The best-known version is the _____. Both are named after Franz Reuleaux, a 19th-century German engineer who did pioneering work on ways that machines translate one type of motion into another, although it was known before his time.
    a. Decagon
    b. Right triangle
    c. Pentagon
    d. Reuleaux triangle

23. A _____ is one of the basic shapes of geometry: a polygon with three corners or vertices and three sides or edges which are line segments. A _____ with vertices A, B, and C is denoted ABC.

In Euclidean geometry any three non-collinear points determine a unique _____ and a unique plane (i.e. a two-dimensional Euclidean space.)

   a. Triangle
   b. -module
   c. 1-center problem
   d. Brocard point

24. In mathematics, two vectors are _____ if they are perpendicular, i.e., they form a right angle. The word comes from the Greek >á½€>ρ>θÏŒ>ς , meaning 'straight', and >>γ>ω>vĪ >α (gonia), meaning 'angle'. For example, a subway and the street above, although they do not physically intersect, are _____ if they cross at a right angle.
   a. Algebraic K-theory
   b. Embedding
   c. Interior algebra
   d. Orthogonal

25. In mathematics, _____ are a family of curves in the plane that intersect a given family of curves at right angles. The problem is classical, but is now understood by means of complex analysis; see for example harmonic conjugate.

For a family of level curves described by g(x,y) = C, where C is a constant, the _____ may be found as the level curves of a new function f(x,y) by solving the partial differential equation

$$\nabla f \cdot \nabla g = 0$$

for f(x,y).

   a. Orthogonal trajectories
   b. Ambient space
   c. Edge
   d. Axis-aligned object

26. In geometry a _____ is traditionally a plane figure that is bounded by a closed path or circuit, composed of a finite sequence of straight line segments (i.e., by a closed polygonal chain.) These segments are called its edges or sides, and the points where two edges meet are the _____'s vertices or corners. The interior of the _____ is sometimes called its body.

Chapter 3. Convexity

a. Right triangle
b. Dodecagon
c. Hexagram
d. Polygon

27. Use of _____ in Real-time imagery. The imaging system calls up the structure of _____ needed for the scene to be created from the database. This is transferred to active memory and finally, to the display system (screen, TV monitors etc) so that the scene can be viewed.
   a. 11-cell
   b. -module
   c. 1-center problem
   d. Polygons

28. A _____ is the path a moving object follows through space. The object might be a projectile or a satellite, for example. It thus includes the meaning of orbit - the path of a planet, an asteroid or a comet as it travels around a central mass.
   a. Trajectory
   b. 11-cell
   c. -module
   d. 1-center problem

29. A connected covering space is a _____ if it is simply connected. The name _____ comes from the following important property: if the mapping $q : D \to X$ is a _____ of the space X and the mapping $p : C \to X$ is any cover of the space X where the covering space C is connected, then there exists a covering map $f : D \to C$ such that $p \circ f = q$. This can be phrased as

The _____ of the space X covers all connected covers of the space X.

   a. AA postulate
   b. ADE classification
   c. Universal cover
   d. ADHM construction

30. In formal mathematical logic, the concept of a _____ may be taken to mean a formula that can be derived according to the derivation rules of a fixed formal system. The statements of a theory as expressed in a formal language are called its elementary _____s and are said to be true.

The essential property of _____s is that they are derivable using a fixed set of inference rules and axioms without any additional assumptions.

a. Proof
b. Rule of inference
c. Theorem
d. Logical axioms

Chapter 4. Modern Euclidean Geometry, Theory, and Applications

1. In geometry, the circumscribed circle or _____ of a polygon is a circle which passes through all the vertices of the polygon. The center of this circle is called the circumcenter.

A polygon which has a circumscribed circle is called a cyclic polygon.

   a. -module
   b. Gergonne point
   c. Circumscribed circle
   d. Circumcircle

2. In geometry, the _____ circle or circumcircle of a polygon is a circle which passes through all the vertices of the polygon. The center of this circle is called the circumcenter.

A polygon which has a _____ circle is called a cyclic polygon.

   a. Circle sector
   b. Circular sector
   c. Circumcenter
   d. Circumscribed

3. In geometry, the _____ or circumcircle of a polygon is a circle which passes through all the vertices of the polygon. The center of this circle is called the circumcenter.

A polygon which has a _____ is called a cyclic polygon.

   a. Circumcircle
   b. -module
   c. Gergonne point
   d. Circumscribed circle

4. In geometry, an _____ system is a set of four points in the plane one of which is the orthocenter of the triangle formed by the other three.

If four points form an _____ system, then each of the four points is the orthocenter of the other three. These four possible triangles will all have the same nine-point circle.

a. Euler line
b. AA postulate
c. Isogonal conjugate
d. Orthocentric

5. A _____ is a simple shape of Euclidean geometry consisting of those points in a plane which are the same distance from a given point called the centre. The common distance of the points of a _____ from its center is called its radius.

_____s are simple closed curves which divide the plane into two regions, an interior and an exterior.

a. Circumcircle
b. Gergonne point
c. Circumscribed circle
d. Circle

6. The _____ of a system of particles is a specific point at which, for many purposes, the system's mass behaves as if it were concentrated. The _____ is a function only of the positions and masses of the particles that comprise the system. In the case of a rigid body, the position of its _____ is fixed in relation to the object (but not necessarily in contact with it.)

a. 11-cell
b. Center of mass
c. -module
d. 1-center problem

7. In geometry, the incircle or inscribed circle of a triangle is the largest circle contained in the triangle; it touches (is tangent to) the three sides. The center of the incircle is called the triangle's _____.

An excircle or escribed circle of the triangle is a circle lying outside the triangle, tangent to one of its sides and tangent to the extensions of the other two.

a. AA postulate
b. Osculating circle
c. Incircle
d. Incenter

Chapter 4. Modern Euclidean Geometry, Theory, and Applications

8. In mathematics, an _____ is the finite or bounded case of a conic section, the geometric shape that results from cutting a circular conical or cylindrical surface with an oblique plane. It is also the locus of all points of the plane whose distances to two fixed points add to the same constant.

_____s also arise as images of a circle or a sphere under parallel projection, and some cases of perspective projection.

a. AA postulate
b. Ellipse
c. ADHM construction
d. ADE classification

9. In geometry, the _____ or inscribed circle of a triangle is the largest circle contained in the triangle; it touches (is tangent to) the three sides. The center of the _____ is called the triangle's incenter.

An excircle or escribed circle of the triangle is a circle lying outside the triangle, tangent to one of its sides and tangent to the extensions of the other two.

a. ADHM construction
b. Incircle
c. ADE classification
d. AA postulate

10. In mathematics, the _____ is a conic section, the intersection of a right circular conical surface and a plane parallel to a generating straight line of that surface. Given a point (the focus) and a line (the directrix) that lie in a plane, the locus of points in that plane that are equidistant to them is a _____.

A particular case arises when the plane is tangent to the conical surface of a circle.

a. 1-center problem
b. -module
c. 11-cell
d. Parabola

11. In geometry, a set of points is said to be _____ if they lie on a common circle. _____ points, showing that the perpendicular bisectors of pairs are concurrent Four _____ points showing that angles >α are the same. Points are the vertices of a cyclic quadrilateral

A circle can be drawn around any triangle.

a. 1-center problem
b. 11-cell
c. -module
d. Concyclic

12. In geometry, a _____ is a quadrilateral whose vertices all lie on a single circle. The vertices are said to be concyclic.

In a _____, opposite angles are supplementary (their sum is >π radians). Equivalently, each exterior angle is equal to the opposite interior angle.

a. Cyclic quadrilateral
b. -module
c. Tangential quadrilateral
d. Rhomboid

13. In geometry, a _____ is a polygon with four 'sides' or edges and four vertices or corners. Sometimes, the term quadrangle is used, for analogy with triangle, and sometimes tetragon for consistency with pentagon (5-sided), hexagon (6-sided) and so on. The word _____ is made of the words quad and lateral.
a. 1-center problem
b. 11-cell
c. -module
d. Quadrilateral

14. _____ is the branch of geometry which makes use of theorems and synthetic observations to draw logical conclusions, as opposed to analytic geometry which uses algebra to perform geometric computations and solve problems.

The process of logical synthesis begins with some arbitrary but defined starting point.

- Primitives are the most basic ideas. Typically they include objects and relationships. In geometry, the objects are things like points, lines, planes and the fundamental relationship is that of incidence - of one object meeting or joining with another.
- Axioms are statements about these primitives, for example that any two points are together incident with just one line (i.e. that for any two points, there is just one line which passes through both of them.)

From a given set of axioms, synthesis proceeds as a carefully constructed logical argument. Where a significant result is proved rigorously, it becomes a theorem.

a. Synthetic geometry
b. 1-center problem
c. 11-cell
d. -module

15. In formal mathematical logic, the concept of a _____ may be taken to mean a formula that can be derived according to the derivation rules of a fixed formal system. The statements of a theory as expressed in a formal language are called its elementary _____s and are said to be true.

The essential property of _____s is that they are derivable using a fixed set of inference rules and axioms without any additional assumptions.

a. Proof
b. Theorem
c. Rule of inference
d. Logical axioms

16. In combinatorial mathematics, given a collection C of sets, a _____ is a set containing exactly one element from each member of the collection: it is a section of the quotient map induced by the collection. If the original sets are not disjoint, there are several different definitions. One variation is that there is a bijection f from the _____ to C such that x is an element of f(x) for each x in the _____.

a. No-three-in-line
b. -module
c. Geometric combinatorics
d. Transversal

17. The _____ of a triangle is the symmedian point of its contact triangle. Denoting the three vertices of the triangle by A, B and C and the three points where the incircle touches the triangle by T_A, T_B and T_C (where T_A is opposite of A, etc.), the triangle $T_A T_B T_C$ is known as the contact triangle or Gergonne triangle of ABC. The incircle of ABC is the circumcircle of $T_A T_B T_C$. The three lines AT_A, BT_B and CT_C intersect in a single point, the triangle's _____ G.

The contact triangle is also called the intouch triangle, and the touchpoints of the excircle with segments BC,CA,AC are the vertices of the extouch triangle.

a. Circumscribed circle
b. -module
c. Circumcircle
d. Gergonne point

18. In geometry, given a triangle and a point on its circumcircle, the intersections formed when lines are constructed from the point perpendicular to each of the triangle's sides are collinear. The line through these points is the _____ however, by William Wallace.

The converse is also true; if the feet of the perpendiculars dropped from a point to the sides of the triangle are collinear, then the point is on the circumcircle.

a. Symmedian point
b. Lemoine point
c. Simson line
d. Symmedian

19. In geometry, topology and related branches of mathematics a spatial _____ describes a specific object within a given space that consists of neither volume, area, length, nor any other higher dimensional analogue. Thus, a _____ is a 0-dimensional object. Because of their nature as one of the simplest geometric concepts, they are often used in one form or another as the fundamental constituents of geometry, physics, vector graphics, and many other fields.

a. Bounded
b. Point
c. 1-center problem
d. -module

20. In geometry, the _____ is a circle that can be constructed for any given triangle. It is so named because it passes through nine significant points, six lying on the triangle itself (unless the triangle is obtuse.) They include:

- The midpoint of each side of the triangle
- The foot of each altitude
- The midpoint of the segment of each altitude from its vertex to the orthocenter (where the three altitudes meet)

The _____ is also known as Feuerbach's circle, Euler's circle, Terquem's circle, the six-points circle, the twelve-points circle, the n-point circle, the medioscribed circle, the mid circle or the circum-midcircle.

Chapter 4. Modern Euclidean Geometry, Theory, and Applications

a. Nine-point circle
b. Circumcenter
c. Circular sector
d. Circle sector

21. In geometry, the _____ is a line determined from any triangle that is not equilateral; it passes through several important points determined from the triangle. In the image, the _____ is shown in red. It passes through the orthocenter (blue), the circumcenter (green), the centroid (orange), and the center of the nine-point circle (red) of the triangle.

a. Orthocentric
b. Isogonal conjugate
c. AA postulate
d. Euler line

22. A _____ is one of the basic shapes of geometry: a polygon with three corners or vertices and three sides or edges which are line segments. A _____ with vertices A, B, and C is denoted ABC.

In Euclidean geometry any three non-collinear points determine a unique _____ and a unique plane (i.e. a two-dimensional Euclidean space.)

a. -module
b. 1-center problem
c. Brocard point
d. Triangle

23. In a group, the _____ by g of h is ghg^{-1}.

If h is a translation, then its _____ by an isometry can be described as applying the isometry to the translation:

- the _____ of a translation by a translation is the first translation
- the _____ of a translation by a rotation is a translation by a rotated translation vector
- the _____ of a translation by a reflection is a translation by a reflected translation vector

Thus the conjugacy class within the Euclidean group E(n) of a translation is the set of all translations by the same distance.

The smallest subgroup of the Euclidean group containing all translations by a given distance is the set of all translations. Thus this is the _____ closure of a singleton containing a translation.

a. 1-center problem
b. 11-cell
c. -module
d. Conjugate

24. In geometry, the _____ of a point P with respect to a triangle ABC is constructed by reflecting the lines PA, PB, and PC about the angle bisectors of A, B, and C. These three reflected lines concur at the _____ of P. (This definition applies only to points not on a sideline of triangle ABC.)

The _____ of a point P is sometimes denoted by P*. The _____ of P* is P.

The _____ of the incentre I is itself.

a. AA postulate
b. Orthocentric
c. Euler line
d. Isogonal conjugate

25. _____s are three particular geometrical lines associated with every triangle. They are constructed by taking a median of the triangle (a line connecting a vertex with the midpoint of the opposite side), and reflecting the line over the corresponding angle bisector (the line through the same vertex that divides the angle of the triangle there in two equal parts.) The three _____s intersect in a single point, the triangle's _____ point or Lemoine point or Grebe point, the latter names coming from >Émile Lemoine, the French mathematician who proved its existence in 1873, and Ernst Wilhelm Grebe who published a paper on it 1847.

a. Symmedian point
b. Simson line
c. Lemoine point
d. Symmedian

26. Symmedians are three particular geometrical lines associated with every triangle. They are constructed by taking a median of the triangle (a line connecting a vertex with the midpoint of the opposite side), and reflecting the line over the corresponding angle bisector (the line through the same vertex that divides the angle of the triangle there in two equal parts.) The three symmedians intersect in a single point, the triangle's _____ or Lemoine point or Grebe point, the latter names coming from >Émile Lemoine, the French mathematician who proved its existence in 1873, and Ernst Wilhelm Grebe who published a paper on it 1847.

Chapter 4. Modern Euclidean Geometry, Theory, and Applications 45

   a. Simson line
   b. Lemoine point
   c. Symmedian
   d. Symmedian point

27. Symmedians are three particular geometrical lines associated with every triangle. They are constructed by taking a median of the triangle (a line connecting a vertex with the midpoint of the opposite side), and reflecting the line over the corresponding angle bisector (the line through the same vertex that divides the angle of the triangle there in two equal parts.) The three symmedians intersect in a single point, the triangle's symmedian point or _____ or Grebe point, the latter names coming from >Émile Lemoine, the French mathematician who proved its existence in 1873, and Ernst Wilhelm Grebe who published a paper on it 1847.
   a. Simson line
   b. Symmedian point
   c. Lemoine point
   d. Symmedian

28. In geometry, the _____ for a triangle is a circle having a diameter of the line segment between the circumcenter and symmedian. It contains the Brocard points. The _____ is named for Henri Brocard.
   a. -module
   b. 1-center problem
   c. Desarguesian plane
   d. Brocard circle

29. In geometry, _____s are special points within a triangle. They are named after Henri Brocard (1845 - 1922), a French mathematician.

In a triangle ABC with sides a, b, and c, where the vertices are labeled A, B and C in counterclockwise order, there is exactly one point P such that the line segments AP, _____, and CP form the same angle, >ω, with the respective sides c, a, and b, namely that

Point P is called the first _____ of the triangle ABC, and the angle >ω is called the Brocard angle of the triangle.

46   Chapter 4. Modern Euclidean Geometry, Theory, and Applications

   a. -module
   b. Brocard point
   c. 11-cell
   d. 1-center problem

30. In mathematics, the _____ are the following sequence of numbers:

$$\ldots$$

By definition, the first two _____ are 0 and 1, and each remaining number is the sum of the previous two. Some sources omit the initial 0, instead beginning the sequence with two 1s.

In mathematical terms, the sequence F_n of _____ is defined by the recurrence relation

$$\ldots$$

with seed values

$$\ldots$$

The Fibonacci sequence is named after Leonardo of Pisa, who was known as Fibonacci (a contraction of filius Bonaccio, 'son of Bonaccio'.)

   a. -module
   b. Fibonacci numbers
   c. 1-center problem
   d. 11-cell

31. In mathematics and the arts, two quantities are in the _____ if the ratio between the sum of those quantities and the larger one is the same as the ratio between the larger one and the smaller. The _____ is an irrational mathematical constant, approximately 1.6180339887.

The _____ is often denoted by the Greek letter phi (>Φ or >φ). The figure of a golden section illustrates the geometric relationship that defines this constant. Expressed algebraically:

$$\ldots$$

a. 11-cell
b. 1-center problem
c. Golden ratio
d. -module

32. A _____ is an expression which compares quantities relative to each other. The most common examples involve two quantities, but in theory any number of quantities can be compared. In mathematical terms, they are represented by separating each quantity with a colon, for example the _____ 2:3, which is read as the _____ 'two to three'.
a. Slope
b. -module
c. Slope of a line
d. Ratio

33. In geometry, a _____ is a logarithmic spiral whose growth factor b is related to φ, the golden ratio. Specifically, a _____ gets wider (or further from its origin) by a factor of φ for every quarter turn it makes.

The polar equation for a _____ is the same as for other logarithmic spirals, but with a special value of b:

or

with e being the base of natural logarithms, a being an arbitrary positive real constant, and b such that when θ is a right angle (a quarter turn in either direction):

Therefore, b is given by

48   Chapter 4. Modern Euclidean Geometry, Theory, and Applications

The numerical value of b depends on whether the right angle is measured as 90 degrees or as [x] radians; and since the angle can be in either direction, it is easiest to write the formula for the absolute value of b (that is, b can also be the negative of this value):

[x] for >θ in degrees;

[x] for >θ in radians.

a. Logarithmic spiral
b. Padovan cuboid spiral
c. Spiral of Theodorus
d. Golden spiral

34. In mathematics, a _____ is a curve which emanates from a central point, getting progressively farther away as it revolves around the point. An Archimedean _____, a helix, and a conic _____.

A '_____' and a 'helix' are two terms that are easily confused, but represent different objects.

A _____ is typically a planar curve (that is, flat), like the groove on a record or the arms of a _____ galaxy.

a. Spiral of Theodorus
b. Logarithmic spiral
c. Cotes' spiral
d. Spiral

35. A _____ or tiling of the plane is a collection of plane figures that fills the plane with no overlaps and no gaps. One may also speak of _____s of the parts of the plane or of other surfaces. Generalizations to higher dimensions are also possible.
a. Tessellation
b. Crystal system
c. Symmetry
d. Screw axis

Chapter 4. Modern Euclidean Geometry, Theory, and Applications

36. In mathematics, especially in geometry and group theory, a _____ in R^n is a discrete subgroup of R^n which spans the real vector space R^n. Every _____ in R^n can be generated from a basis for the vector space by forming all linear combinations with integral coefficients. A _____ may be viewed as a regular tiling of a space by a primitive cell.
   a. -module
   b. 1-center problem
   c. Bounded
   d. Lattice

37. The vectors p and q can be represented by complex numbers. Up to size and orientation, a pair can be represented by their quotient. Expressed geometrically: if two _____ s are 0 and 1, we consider the position of a third _____.
   a. 11-cell
   b. Lattice point
   c. -module
   d. 1-center problem

38. Problems of the following type, and their solution techniques, were first studied in the nineteenth century, and the general topic became known as _____.

   - (Buffon's needle) What is the chance that a needle dropped randomly onto a floor marked with equally spaced parallel lines will cross one of the lines?

   - What is the mean length of a random chord of a unit circle? (cf. Bertrand's paradox.)

   - What is the chance that three random points in the plane form an acute (rather than obtuse) triangle?

   - What is the mean area of the polygonal regions formed when randomly-oriented lines are spread over the plane?

   For mathematical development see the concise monograph Solomon.

   Since the late twentieth century the topic has split into two topics with different emphases.

   a. Lateral surface
   b. Coxeter group
   c. Geometric probability
   d. Lipschitz domain

39. _____ are sets whose elements have degrees of membership. _____ were introduced by Lotfi A. Zadeh (1965) as an extension of the classical notion of set. In classical set theory, the membership of elements in a set is assessed in binary terms according to a bivalent condition -- an element either belongs or does not belong to the set.

a. 1-center problem
b. -module
c. 11-cell
d. Fuzzy sets

40. _____ are a class of computational algorithms that rely on repeated random sampling to compute their results. _____ are often used when simulating physical and mathematical systems. Because of their reliance on repeated computation and random or pseudo-random numbers, _____ are most suited to calculation by a computer.

a. 1-center problem
b. Monte Carlo methods
c. -module
d. 11-cell

41. In mathematical analysis and related areas of mathematics, a set is called _____, if it is, in a certain sense, of finite size. Conversely a set which is not _____ is called unbounded.

A set S of real numbers is called _____ from above if there is a real number k such that k >≥ s for all s in S. The number k is called an upper bound of S. The terms _____ from below and lower bound are similarly defined.

a. 11-cell
b. 1-center problem
c. -module
d. Bounded

42. _____ is a term used in robotics for the process of detailing a task into atomic motions.

For example, consider navigating a mobile robot inside a building to a distant waypoint. It should execute this task while avoiding walls and not falling down stairs.

a. Motion planning
b. 1-center problem
c. 11-cell
d. -module

Chapter 4. Modern Euclidean Geometry, Theory, and Applications

43. In geometry a _____ is traditionally a plane figure that is bounded by a closed path or circuit, composed of a finite sequence of straight line segments (i.e., by a closed polygonal chain.) These segments are called its edges or sides, and the points where two edges meet are the _____'s vertices or corners. The interior of the _____ is sometimes called its body.
   a. Polygon
   b. Dodecagon
   c. Hexagram
   d. Right triangle

44. Use of _____ in Real-time imagery. The imaging system calls up the structure of _____ needed for the scene to be created from the database. This is transferred to active memory and finally, to the display system (screen, TV monitors etc) so that the scene can be viewed.
   a. 1-center problem
   b. Polygons
   c. -module
   d. 11-cell

45. In numerical analysis, a _____ is the interpolating polynomial for a given set of data points in the Lagrange form. It was first discovered by Edward Waring in 1779 and later rediscovered by Leonhard Euler in 1783.

   Notice that, for any given set of data points, there is only one polynomial that interpolates these points.

   a. Lagrange polynomial
   b. -module
   c. 11-cell
   d. 1-center problem

46. In mathematics, a _____ consists of the points through which a continuously moving point passes. This notion captures the intuitive idea of a geometrical one-dimensional object, which furthermore is connected in the sense of having no discontinuities or gaps. Simple examples include the sine wave as the basic _____ underlying simple harmonic motion, and the parabola.
   a. Dual curve
   b. Curve
   c. Sectrix of Maclaurin
   d. Singular point

Chapter 5. Constructions

1. A _____, magnetic _____ or mariner's _____ is a navigational instrument for determining direction relative to the earth's magnetic poles. It consists of a magnetized pointer (usually marked on the North end) free to align itself with Earth's magnetic field. The _____ greatly improved the safety and efficiency of travel, especially ocean travel.
    a. 1-center problem
    b. 11-cell
    c. -module
    d. Compass

2. A _____ is a tool with an accurately straight edge used for drawing or cutting straight lines, or checking the straightness of lines. If it has equally spaced markings along its length it is usually called a ruler.

    True straightness can in some cases be checked by using a laser line level as an optical _____: it can illuminate an accurately straight line on a flat surface such as the edge of a plank or shelf.

    a. Spirit level
    b. Straightedge
    c. Machinist square
    d. Feeler gauge

3. In geometry, two sets of points are called _____ if one can be transformed into the other by an isometry, i.e., a combination of translations, rotations and reflections. Less formally, two figures are _____ if they have the same shape and size, but are in different positions (for instance one may be rotated, flipped, or simply placed somewhere else).
    a. 1-center problem
    b. -module
    c. Bounded
    d. Congruent

4. In mathematical analysis and related areas of mathematics, a set is called _____, if it is, in a certain sense, of finite size. Conversely a set which is not _____ is called unbounded.

    A set S of real numbers is called _____ from above if there is a real number k such that k >≥ s for all s in S. The number k is called an upper bound of S. The terms _____ from below and lower bound are similarly defined.

    a. -module
    b. 1-center problem
    c. Bounded
    d. 11-cell

Chapter 5. Constructions 53

5. A point in the Euclidean plane is a constructible point if, given a fixed coordinate system (or a fixed line segment of unit length), the point can be constructed with unruled straightedge and compass. A complex number is a _____ if its corresponding point in the Euclidean plane is constructible from the usual x- and y-coordinate axes.

It can then be shown that a real number is constructible if and only if, given a line segment of unit length, a line segment of length $|r|$ can be constructed with compass and straightedge.

   a. Constructible number
   b. Philo line
   c. Special right triangle
   d. Tilings by regular polygons

6. A _____ is one of the basic shapes of geometry: a polygon with three corners or vertices and three sides or edges which are line segments. A _____ with vertices A, B, and C is denoted ABC.

In Euclidean geometry any three non-collinear points determine a unique _____ and a unique plane (i.e. a two-dimensional Euclidean space.)

   a. Brocard point
   b. 1-center problem
   c. -module
   d. Triangle

7. In mathematics, two vectors are _____ if they are perpendicular, i.e., they form a right angle. The word comes from the Greek >á½€>ρ>θϏŒ>ς , meaning 'straight', and >>γ>ω>vϏ>α (gonia), meaning 'angle'. For example, a subway and the street above, although they do not physically intersect, are _____ if they cross at a right angle.
   a. Algebraic K-theory
   b. Embedding
   c. Interior algebra
   d. Orthogonal

8. In mathematics, a _____ consists of the points through which a continuously moving point passes. This notion captures the intuitive idea of a geometrical one-dimensional object, which furthermore is connected in the sense of having no discontinuities or gaps. Simple examples include the sine wave as the basic _____ underlying simple harmonic motion, and the parabola.

a. Dual curve
b. Sectrix of Maclaurin
c. Curve
d. Singular point

9. In mathematics, a _____ is a convincing demonstration (within the accepted standards of the field) that some mathematical statement is necessarily true. _____s are obtained from deductive reasoning, rather than from inductive or empirical arguments. That is, a _____ must demonstrate that a statement is true in all cases, without a single exception.
a. Proof
b. Logical axioms
c. Contrapositive
d. Theorem

10. In geometry and trigonometry, an _____ is the figure formed by two rays sharing a common endpoint, called the vertex of the _____ . The magnitude of the _____ is the 'amount of rotation' that separates the two rays, and can be measured by considering the length of circular arc swept out when one ray is rotated about the vertex to coincide with the other Where there is no possibility of confusion, the term '_____' is used interchangeably for both the geometric configuration itself and for its angular magnitude (which is simply a numerical quantity.)
a. AA postulate
b. ADHM construction
c. ADE classification
d. Angle

11. A _____ is a simple shape of Euclidean geometry consisting of those points in a plane which are the same distance from a given point called the centre. The common distance of the points of a _____ from its center is called its radius.

_____s are simple closed curves which divide the plane into two regions, an interior and an exterior.

a. Gergonne point
b. Circumscribed circle
c. Circumcircle
d. Circle

Chapter 5. Constructions

12. In mathematics, an _____ is a complex number that is a root of a non-zero polynomial in one variable with rational (or equivalently, integer) coefficients. Numbers such as pi that are not algebraic are said to be transcendental, and are infinitely more numerous within the complex number field.

- The rational numbers, those expressed as the ratio of two whole numbers b and a, a not equal to zero, satisfy the above definition because x = >− b / a is derived from (and satisfies) ax + b = 0. (In general, a or b can be negative, as can x.)

- Some irrational numbers are algebraic and some are not:

    - The numbers ☐ > and ☐ > are algebraic since they are the roots of x^2 >− 2 = 0 and $8x^3$ >− 3 = 0, respectively.

    - The golden ratio >φ is algebraic since it is a root of the polynomial x^2 >− x >− 1 = 0.

    - The numbers >π and e are not _____s ; hence they are transcendental.

- The constructible numbers (those that, starting with a unit, can be constructed with straightedge and compass, e.g. the square root of 2) are algebraic.

- The quadratic surds (roots of a quadratic equation ax^2 + bx + c = 0 with integer coefficients a, b, and c) are _____s. If the quadratic equation is monic (the leading coefficient a = 1) then the roots are quadratic integers.

a. Associativity
b. Algebraic number
c. Associative
d. AA postulate

13. A _____ is a curve derived from a fixed point O, another curve, and a length d. For every line through O that intersects the given curve at A the two points on the line which are d from A are on the _____.

The simplest expression uses polar coordinates with O at the origin. If r = >α(>θ) expresses the given curve then ☐ > expresses the _____.

a. Conchoid
b. Brachistochrone curve
c. Cycloid
d. Trochoid

14. In mathematics, a _____ is a curve which emanates from a central point, getting progressively farther away as it revolves around the point. An Archimedean _____, a helix, and a conic _____.

A '_____' and a 'helix' are two terms that are easily confused, but represent different objects.

A _____ is typically a planar curve (that is, flat), like the groove on a record or the arms of a _____ galaxy.

   a. Logarithmic spiral
   b. Spiral of Theodorus
   c. Cotes' spiral
   d. Spiral

15. In geometry, two lines or planes (or a line and a plane), are considered _____ to each other if they form congruent adjacent angles (an L-shape.) The term may be used as a noun or adjective. Thus, referring to Figure 1, the line AB is the _____ to CD through the point B. Note that by definition, a line is infinitely long, and strictly speaking AB and CD in this example represent line segments of two infinitely long lines.
   a. Perpendicular
   b. Heilbronn triangle problem
   c. Partial linear space
   d. Point group in two dimensions

16. In geometry, bisection is the division of something into two equal or congruent parts, usually by a line, which is then called a bisector. The most often considered types of bisectors are segment bisectors and angle bisectors. Bisection of a line segment using a compass and ruler Bisection of an angle using a compass and ruler Line DE bisects line AB at D, line EF is a _____ of segment AD at C and the interior bisector of right angle AED

A line segment bisector passes through the midpoint of the segment.

   a. Perpendicular Bisector
   b. Concyclic
   c. -module
   d. 1-center problem

17. _____ are a class of computational algorithms that rely on repeated random sampling to compute their results. _____ are often used when simulating physical and mathematical systems. Because of their reliance on repeated computation and random or pseudo-random numbers, _____ are most suited to calculation by a computer.

a. 1-center problem
b. -module
c. 11-cell
d. Monte Carlo methods

18. In geometry, topology and related branches of mathematics a spatial _____ describes a specific object within a given space that consists of neither volume, area, length, nor any other higher dimensional analogue. Thus, a _____ is a 0-dimensional object. Because of their nature as one of the simplest geometric concepts, they are often used in one form or another as the fundamental constituents of geometry, physics, vector graphics, and many other fields.

a. 1-center problem
b. Bounded
c. Point
d. -module

19. In formal mathematical logic, the concept of a _____ may be taken to mean a formula that can be derived according to the derivation rules of a fixed formal system. The statements of a theory as expressed in a formal language are called its elementary _____s and are said to be true.

The essential property of _____s is that they are derivable using a fixed set of inference rules and axioms without any additional assumptions.

a. Proof
b. Theorem
c. Rule of inference
d. Logical axioms

Chapter 6. The Transformation of Inversion

1. _____ are a natural extension of Poincar>é transformations to include all conformal one-to-one transformations on coordinate space-time. They are less studied in physics because unlike the rotations and translations of Poincar>é symmetry an object cannot be physically transformed by the inversion symmetry. Some physical theories are invariant under this symmetry, in these cases it is what is known as a 'hidden symmetry'.

   a. ADHM construction
   b. AA postulate
   c. Inversion transformations
   d. ADE classification

2. In mathematics, a _____ could be any function mapping a set X onto another set or onto itself. However, often the set X has some additional algebraic or geometric structure and the term '_____' refers to a function from X to itself which preserves this structure.

   Examples include linear _____s and affine _____s such as rotations, reflections and translations.

   a. Codomain
   b. -module
   c. 1-center problem
   d. Transformation

3. A _____ is a simple shape of Euclidean geometry consisting of those points in a plane which are the same distance from a given point called the centre. The common distance of the points of a _____ from its center is called its radius.

   _____s are simple closed curves which divide the plane into two regions, an interior and an exterior.

   a. Circumscribed circle
   b. Circumcircle
   c. Circle
   d. Gergonne point

4. An _____ is a class of incidence structure in mathematics.

   It may be axiomatised by taking two classes, 'points' and 'circles' (or 'blocks') with the properties

   - any three points lie on exactly one circle;
   - if P and Q are points and c a circle with P on c and Q not, then there is exactly one circle e containing P and Q and intersecting c only in P;
   - there are four points not all on the same circle.

The finite _____s are precisely the 3 >− (n^2 + 1, n + 1, 1) >− designs. Such a design is always a Steiner system.

When one takes as points the points of an ovoid in PG(3,q), with q a prime power, and as blocks the planes that are not tangent to the ovoid, one finds a 3 >− (q^2 + 1, q + 1, 1) >− design.

a. AA postulate
b. ADE classification
c. Inversive plane
d. ADHM construction

5. In mathematics, a _____ is a flat surface. _____s can arise as subspaces of some higher dimensional space, as with the walls of a room, or they may enjoy an independent existence in their own right, as in the setting of Euclidean geometry
a. Pendent
b. Parallelogram law
c. Simple polytope
d. Plane

6. In geometry, topology and related branches of mathematics a spatial _____ describes a specific object within a given space that consists of neither volume, area, length, nor any other higher dimensional analogue. Thus, a _____ is a 0-dimensional object. Because of their nature as one of the simplest geometric concepts, they are often used in one form or another as the fundamental constituents of geometry, physics, vector graphics, and many other fields.
a. Bounded
b. -module
c. 1-center problem
d. Point

7. In mathematics, a _____ is a number that can be expressed as an integral of an algebraic function over an algebraic domain. The concept has been promoted by Maxim Kontsevich and Don Zagier.

In elementary mathematics each group of three digits in a number is called a _____

a. -module
b. 1-center problem
c. Bounded
d. Period

8. In mathematics, two vectors are _____ if they are perpendicular, i.e., they form a right angle. The word comes from the Greek >á½€>ρ>θÏŒ>ς , meaning 'straight', and >>γ>ω>vΐ >α (gonia), meaning 'angle'. For example, a subway and the street above, although they do not physically intersect, are _____ if they cross at a right angle.
   a. Interior algebra
   b. Embedding
   c. Algebraic K-theory
   d. Orthogonal

9. In kinematics, Euler's rotation theorem states that, in three-dimensional space, any displacement of a rigid body such that a point on the rigid body remains fixed, is equivalent to a rotation about a fixed axis through that point. The theorem is named after Leonhard Euler, who proved this in 1775 by an elementary geometric argument. The axis of rotation is known as an _____.
   a. ADHM construction
   b. ADE classification
   c. AA postulate
   d. Euler pole

10. In geometry, the terms _____ and polar are used to describe a point and a line that have a unique reciprocal relationship with respect to a given conic section. If the point lies on the conic section, its polar is the tangent line to the conic section at that point.

For a given circle, the operation of reciprocation in a circle corresponds to transforming each point in the plane into its polar line and each line in the plane into its _____.

   a. 1-center problem
   b. 11-cell
   c. -module
   d. Pole

11. _____, usually called coordinate geometry and earlier referred to as Cartesian geometry or analytical geometry, is the study of geometry using the principles of algebra; the modern development of _____ is thus suggestively called algebraic geometry.

Chapter 6. The Transformation of Inversion

Usually the Cartesian coordinate system is applied to manipulate equations for planes, straight lines, and squares, often in two and sometimes in three dimensions of measurement. Geometrical, one studies the Euclidean plane (2 dimensions) and Euclidean space (3 dimensions.)

   a. Equable shape
   b. Analytic geometry
   c. Apothem
   d. Infinitely near point

12. In geometry, a _____ is a three-dimensional element that is part of a higher-dimensional object.

A _____ is a three-dimensional polyhedron element that is part of the boundary of a higher-dimensional polytope, such as a polychoron (4-polytope) or honeycomb (3-space tessellation.)

For example, a cubic honeycomb is made of cubic _____s, with 4 cubes on each edge.

   a. Stack
   b. General position
   c. Gyroid
   d. Cell

13. In geometry, the _____ is a circle that can be constructed for any given triangle. It is so named because it passes through nine significant points, six lying on the triangle itself (unless the triangle is obtuse.) They include:

   - The midpoint of each side of the triangle
   - The foot of each altitude
   - The midpoint of the segment of each altitude from its vertex to the orthocenter (where the three altitudes meet)

The _____ is also known as Feuerbach's circle, Euler's circle, Terquem's circle, the six-points circle, the twelve-points circle, the n-point circle, the medioscribed circle, the mid circle or the circum-midcircle.

   a. Nine-point circle
   b. Circumcenter
   c. Circular sector
   d. Circle sector

14. In mathematics, a _____ is a convincing demonstration (within the accepted standards of the field) that some mathematical statement is necessarily true. _____s are obtained from deductive reasoning, rather than from inductive or empirical arguments. That is, a _____ must demonstrate that a statement is true in all cases, without a single exception.
   a. Contrapositive
   b. Logical axioms
   c. Theorem
   d. Proof

15. In formal mathematical logic, the concept of a _____ may be taken to mean a formula that can be derived according to the derivation rules of a fixed formal system. The statements of a theory as expressed in a formal language are called its elementary _____s and are said to be true.

The essential property of _____s is that they are derivable using a fixed set of inference rules and axioms without any additional assumptions.

   a. Theorem
   b. Rule of inference
   c. Logical axioms
   d. Proof

16. In mathematics, _____ is a non-Euclidean geometry, meaning that the parallel postulate of Euclidean geometry is replaced. The parallel postulate in Euclidean geometry is equivalent to the statement that, in two dimensional space, for any given line l and point P not on l, there is exactly one line through P that does not intersect l; i.e., that is parallel to l. In _____ there are at least two distinct lines through P which do not intersect l, so the parallel postulate is false.
   a. Tameness conjecture
   b. Complex geodesic
   c. Margulis lemma
   d. Hyperbolic geometry

17. In geometry, the _____ is a particular mapping (function) that projects a sphere onto a plane. The projection is defined on the entire sphere, except at one point -- the projection point. Where it is defined, the mapping is smooth and bijective.
   a. 1-center problem
   b. Stereographic projection
   c. Mercator projection
   d. -module

Chapter 7. Projective Geometry

1. In mathematics _____ is the study of geometric properties which are invariant under projective transformations. The field of _____ is itself divided into many subfields, two examples of which are projective algebraic geometry (the study of projective varieties) and projective differential geometry (the study of differential invariants of the projective transformations.)

_____, like affine and Euclidean geometry, can be developed from the Erlangen program of Felix Klein.

a. Geometric probability
b. John ellipsoid
c. Birational geometry
d. Projective geometry

2. In chemistry, the _____ molecular geometry describes the arrangement of three or more atoms placed at an expected bond angle of 180°. _____ organic molecules, e.g. acetylene, are often described by invoking sp orbital hybridization for the carbon centers. Many _____ molecules exist, prominent examples include CO_2, HCN, and xenon difluoride.

a. Linear
b. -module
c. 11-cell
d. 1-center problem

3. Perspective in the graphic arts, such as drawing, is an approximate representation, on a flat surface, of an image as it is perceived by the eye. The two most characteristic features of perspective are that objects are drawn:

- Smaller as their distance from the observer increases
- Foreshortened: the size of an object's dimensions along the line of sight are relatively shorter than dimensions across the line of sight

A cube in two-point perspective. Rays of light travel from the object, through the picture plane, and to the viewer's eye. This is the basis for graphical perspective.

_____ works by representing the light that passes from a scene through an imaginary rectangle (the painting), to the viewer's eye. It is similar to a viewer looking through a window and painting what is seen directly onto the windowpane.

a. 1-center problem
b. -module
c. 11-cell
d. Linear perspective

Chapter 7. Projective Geometry

4. _____ is the study and practice of making geographical maps. Combining science, aesthetics, and technique, _____ builds on the premise that reality can be modeled in ways that communicate spatial information effectively.

The fundamental problems of _____ are to:

- Set the map's agenda and select traits of the object to be mapped. This is the concern of map editing. Traits may be physical, such as roads or land masses, or may be abstract, such as toponyms or political boundaries.
- Represent the terrain of the mapped object on flat media. This is the concern of map projections.
- Eliminate characteristics of the mapped object that are not relevant to the map's purpose. This is the concern of generalization.
- Reduce the complexity of the characteristics that will be mapped. This is also the concern of generalization.
- Orchestrate the elements of the map to best convey its message to its audience. This is the concern of map design.

Copy (1475) of St. Isidore's TO map of the world.

The earliest known map is a matter of some debate, both because the definition of 'map' is not sharp and because some artifacts speculated to be maps might actually be something else. A wall painting, which may depict the ancient Anatolian city of >Çatalh>öy>ük (previously known as Catal Huyuk or >Çatal H>üy>ük), has been dated to the late 7th millennium BCE. Other known maps of the ancient world include the Minoan 'House of the Admiral' wall painting from c.

a. 11-cell
b. -module
c. 1-center problem
d. Cartography

5. A _____ is a family of geometric objects, such as lines, that have a common property, such as passage through a given line in a given plane.

In more technical language, a _____ is the special case of a linear system of divisors in which the parameter space is a projective line. Typical _____s of curves in the projective plane, for example, are written as

$$\lambda C + \mu C' = 0$$

where

$$C = 0, C' = 0$$

are plane curves.

Chapter 7. Projective Geometry 65

a. Hyperplane section
b. Borel fixed-point theorem
c. Nakai conjecture
d. Pencil

6. In geometry, topology and related branches of mathematics a spatial _____ describes a specific object within a given space that consists of neither volume, area, length, nor any other higher dimensional analogue. Thus, a _____ is a 0-dimensional object. Because of their nature as one of the simplest geometric concepts, they are often used in one form or another as the fundamental constituents of geometry, physics, vector graphics, and many other fields.

a. Bounded
b. 1-center problem
c. -module
d. Point

7. In mathematics, specifically projective geometry, a _____ is a projective configuration $(4_3 6_2)$ consisting of four points, no three of which are collinear, and the six lines defined by those four points. This configuration was called a tetrastigm by Lachlan (1893), and that term is occasionally still used. The projective dual configuration $(6_2 4_3)$ to a _____ is a complete quadrilateral (called a tetragram by Lachlan), a configuration consisting of four lines, no three of which pass through a common point, and the six points of intersection of those four lines.

a. Projective transformation
b. Projective space
c. Cross ratio
d. Complete quadrangle

8. In the field of mathematical logic, a clear distinction is made between two notions of axioms: _____ and non-_____

These are certain formulas in a formal language that are universally valid, that is, formulas that are satisfied by every assignment of values. Usually one takes as _____ at least some minimal set of tautologies that is sufficient for proving all tautologies in the language; in the case of predicate logic more _____ than that are required, in order to prove logical truths that are not tautologies in the strict sense.

In propositional logic it is common to take as _____ all formulae of the following forms, where φ, χ, and ψ can be any formulae of the language and where the included primitive connectives are only '¬' for negation of the immediately following proposition and '→' for implication from antecedent to consequent propositions:

1. $\phi \to (\psi \to \phi)$
2. $(\phi \to (\psi \to \chi)) \to ((\phi \to \psi) \to (\phi \to \chi))$
3. $(\neg\phi \to \neg\psi) \to (\psi \to \phi)$.

Each of these patterns is an axiom schema, a rule for generating an infinite number of axioms. For example, if A, B, and C are propositional variables, then $A \to (B \to A)$ and $(A \to \neg B) \to (C \to (A \to \neg B))$ are both instances of axiom schema 1, and hence are axioms.

a. Logically equivalent
b. Contrapositive
c. Theorem
d. Logical axioms

9. In the field of mathematical logic, a clear distinction is made between two notions of _____s: logical _____s and non-logical _____s (somewhat similar to the ancient distinction between '_____s' and 'postulates' respectively)

These are certain formulas in a formal language that are universally valid, that is, formulas that are satisfied by every assignment of values. Usually one takes as logical _____s at least some minimal set of tautologies that is sufficient for proving all tautologies in the language; in the case of predicate logic more logical _____s than that are required, in order to prove logical truths that are not tautologies in the strict sense.

In propositional logic it is common to take as logical _____s all formulae of the following forms, where φ, χ, and ψ can be any formulae of the language and where the included primitive connectives are only '¬' for negation of the immediately following proposition and '→' for implication from antecedent to consequent propositions:

1. $\phi \to (\psi \to \phi)$
2. $(\phi \to (\psi \to \chi)) \to ((\phi \to \psi) \to (\phi \to \chi))$
3. $(\neg\phi \to \neg\psi) \to (\psi \to \phi)$.

Each of these patterns is an _____ schema, a rule for generating an infinite number of _____s. For example, if A, B, and C are propositional variables, then $A \to (B \to A)$ and $(A \to \neg B) \to (C \to (A \to \neg B))$ are both instances of _____ schema 1, and hence are _____s.

a. Inductive reasoning
b. AA postulate
c. Axiom
d. ADE classification

10. A _____ is one of the basic shapes of geometry: a polygon with three corners or vertices and three sides or edges which are line segments. A _____ with vertices A, B, and C is denoted ABC.

In Euclidean geometry any three non-collinear points determine a unique _____ and a unique plane (i.e. a two-dimensional Euclidean space.)

a. Brocard point
b. -module
c. 1-center problem
d. Triangle

11. In mathematics _____ is the study of geometric properties which remain unchanged by affine transformations, i.e. non-singular linear transformations and translations. The name _____, like projective geometry and Euclidean geometry, follows naturally from the Erlangen program of Felix Klein.

_____ is a form of geometry featuring the unique parallel line property where the notion of angle is undefined and lengths cannot be compared in different directions (that is, Euclid's third and fourth postulates are meaningless.)

a. Ordered geometry
b. Affine geometry
c. Analytic geometry
d. Angular eccentricity

12. In geometry, an _____ or affine map or an affinity between two vector spaces consists of a linear transformation followed by a translation:

$x \mapsto$

In the finite-dimensional case each _____ is given by a matrix A and a vector b, satisfying certain properties described below.

Geometrically, an _____ in Euclidean space is one that preserves

1. The collinearity relation between points; i.e., three points which lie on a line continue to be collinear after the transformation
2. Ratios of distances along a line; i.e., for distinct collinear points p_1, p_2, p_3, the ratio $|p_2 - p_1| / |p_3 - p_2|$ is preserved

In general, an affine transform is composed of linear transformations (rotation, scaling or shear) and a translation (or 'shift'.) Several linear transformations can be combined into a single one, so that the general formula given above is still applicable.

Ordinary vector algebra uses matrix multiplication to represent linear transformations, and vector addition to represent translations.

a. Affine hull
b. Affine group
c. Oblique reflections
d. Affine transformation

13. In mathematics, especially in geometry and group theory, a _____ in R^n is a discrete subgroup of R^n which spans the real vector space R^n. Every _____ in R^n can be generated from a basis for the vector space by forming all linear combinations with integral coefficients. A _____ may be viewed as a regular tiling of a space by a primitive cell.
a. Bounded
b. -module
c. 1-center problem
d. Lattice

14. In mathematics, the _____, sometimes referred to as the fourth isomorphism theorem or the correspondence theorem, states that there exists a bijection from the set of all subgroups of a group G that contain a normal subgroup N onto the set of all subgroups of the quotient group G / N. This means that the structure of the subgroups of G / N is exactly the same as the structure of the subgroups of G containing N, with N collapsed to the identity element.

This establishes an antitone Galois connection between the lattice of subgroups of G and the lattice of subgroups of G / N, where the associated closure operator on subgroups of G is [x] >

Specifically, for a group G and a normal subgroup N of G, there exists a bijection from the set of all subgroups A of G containing N onto the set of subgroups A' of G / N that maps a subgroup A of G to a subgroup A' = A / N of G / N.

a. 1-center problem
b. 11-cell
c. -module
d. Lattice theorem

15. In mathematics, a _____ could be any function mapping a set X onto another set or onto itself. However, often the set X has some additional algebraic or geometric structure and the term '_____' refers to a function from X to itself which preserves this structure.

Examples include linear _____s and affine _____s such as rotations, reflections and translations.

a. Transformation
b. -module
c. 1-center problem
d. Codomain

16. In formal mathematical logic, the concept of a _____ may be taken to mean a formula that can be derived according to the derivation rules of a fixed formal system. The statements of a theory as expressed in a formal language are called its elementary _____s and are said to be true.

The essential property of _____s is that they are derivable using a fixed set of inference rules and axioms without any additional assumptions.

a. Proof
b. Rule of inference
c. Logical axioms
d. Theorem

17. In mathematics, a _____ is a flat surface. _____s can arise as subspaces of some higher dimensional space, as with the walls of a room, or they may enjoy an independent existence in their own right, as in the setting of Euclidean geometry
a. Parallelogram law
b. Plane
c. Pendent
d. Simple polytope

Chapter 7. Projective Geometry

18. In mathematics, specifically projective geometry, a complete quadrangle is a projective configuration ($4_3 6_2$) consisting of four points, no three of which are collinear, and the six lines defined by those four points. This configuration was called a tetrastigm by Lachlan (1893), and that term is occasionally still used. The projective dual configuration ($6_2 4_3$) to a complete quadrangle is a _____, a configuration consisting of four lines, no three of which pass through a common point, and the six points of intersection of those four lines.
   a. Cross ratio
   b. Projective transformation
   c. Projective space
   d. Complete quadrilateral

19. In geometry, a _____ is a polygon with four 'sides' or edges and four vertices or corners. Sometimes, the term quadrangle is used, for analogy with triangle, and sometimes tetragon for consistency with pentagon (5-sided), hexagon (6-sided) and so on. The word _____ is made of the words quad and lateral.
   a. -module
   b. 11-cell
   c. 1-center problem
   d. Quadrilateral

20. _____ is the boundless, three-dimensional extent in which objects and events occur and have relative position and direction. Physical _____ is often conceived in three linear dimensions, although modern physicists usually consider it, with time, to be part of the boundless four-dimensional continuum known as spacetime. In mathematics _____s with different numbers of dimensions and with different underlying structures can be examined.
   a. 1-center problem
   b. 11-cell
   c. -module
   d. Space

21. In mathematics, especially geometry, a _____ is an arrangement of points in a certain way.
   a. 1-center problem
   b. Synthetic geometry
   c. -module
   d. Configuration

22. In mathematical analysis and related areas of mathematics, a set is called _____, if it is, in a certain sense, of finite size. Conversely a set which is not _____ is called unbounded.

Chapter 7. Projective Geometry 71

A set S of real numbers is called _____ from above if there is a real number k such that k >≥ s for all s in S. The number k is called an upper bound of S. The terms _____ from below and lower bound are similarly defined.

a. 1-center problem
b. 11-cell
c. -module
d. Bounded

23. In a group, the _____ by g of h is ghg^{-1}.

If h is a translation, then its _____ by an isometry can be described as applying the isometry to the translation:

- the _____ of a translation by a translation is the first translation
- the _____ of a translation by a rotation is a translation by a rotated translation vector
- the _____ of a translation by a reflection is a translation by a reflected translation vector

Thus the conjugacy class within the Euclidean group E(n) of a translation is the set of all translations by the same distance.

The smallest subgroup of the Euclidean group containing all translations by a given distance is the set of all translations. Thus this is the _____ closure of a singleton containing a translation.

a. -module
b. 1-center problem
c. 11-cell
d. Conjugate

24. In mathematics, the _____ of a harmonic real-valued function of two variables u(x,y), is a function v(x,y) such that v is harmonic and u and v satisfy the Cauchy-Riemann equations. If the Cauchy-Riemann equations are satisfied and all four partial derivatives of u and v are continuous, then the complex-valued function u(x,y) + iv(x,y) = f(z) is analytic. The _____ is unique up to addition of a constant to v.

For example, consider the function

Since

$$\boxed{x}>$$

and

$$\boxed{x}>$$

it satisfies

$$\boxed{x}>$$

and thus is harmonic.

a. 1-center problem
b. 11-cell
c. -module
d. Harmonic conjugate

25. In statistics, _____ indicates the strength and direction of a linear relationship between two random variables. That is in contrast with the usage of the term in colloquial speech, which denotes any relationship, not necessarily linear. In general statistical usage, _____ or co-relation refers to the departure of two random variables from independence.
a. Correlation
b. 11-cell
c. -module
d. 1-center problem

26. A _____ is a transformation used in projective geometry: it is the composition of a pair of perspective projections. It describes what happens to the perceived positions of observed objects when the point of view of the observer changes.
_____s do not preserve sizes or angles but do preserve incidence and cross-ratio: two properties which are important in projective geometry.
a. Projective space
b. Projective transformation
c. Cross-ratio
d. Cross ratio

Chapter 7. Projective Geometry

27. In category theory, a branch of mathematics, duality is a correspondence between properties of a category C and so-called _____ properties of the opposite category C^{op}. Given a statement regarding the category C, by interchanging the source and target of each morphism as well as interchanging the order of composing two morphisms, a corresponding _____ statement is obtained regarding the opposite category C^{op}. Duality, as such, is the assertion that truth is invariant under this operation on statements.

a. 11-cell
b. 1-center problem
c. -module
d. Dual

28. A _____ is a number that determines the location of a point along some line or curve. A list of two, three, or more _____ s can be used to determine the location of a point on a surface, volume, or higher-dimensional domain.

For example, the longitude is a _____ which determines the position of a point along the Earth's equator, and latitude is another _____ that defines a poisition along a meridian.

a. 1-center problem
b. 11-cell
c. -module
d. Coordinate

29. In mathematics, _____, introduced by August Ferdinand M>öbius in his 1827 work Der barycentrische Calc>ül, make calculations possible in projective space just as Cartesian coordinates do in Euclidean space. _____ have a range of applications, including to computer graphics where they allow affine transformations and, in general, projective transformations to be easily represented by a matrix.

The _____ of a point of projective space of dimension n are usually written as (x : y : z : ...

a. Homogeneous coordinates
b. -module
c. 11-cell
d. 1-center problem

30. In finite geometry a _____ is a plane in which Desargues' theorem holds. The ordinary real projective plane is a _____. More generally any projective plane over a division ring is Desarguesian, and conversely Hilbert showed that any Desarguesan projective plane is the projective plane over some division ring.

Chapter 7. Projective Geometry

a. 1-center problem
b. Desarguesian plane
c. Brocard circle
d. -module

31. Arthur Cayley and Felix Klein found an application of the cross-ratio to non-Euclidean geometry. Given a nonsingular conic C in the real projective plane, its stabilizer G in the projective group PGL(3,R) acts transitively on the points in the interior of C. However, there is an invariant for the action of G on the pairs of points. In fact, every such invariant is expressible as a function of the appropriate _____.
a. Cross-ratio
b. Cross ratio
c. Projective space
d. Projective transformation

32. A _____ is an expression which compares quantities relative to each other. The most common examples involve two quantities, but in theory any number of quantities can be compared. In mathematical terms, they are represented by separating each quantity with a colon, for example the _____ 2:3, which is read as the _____ 'two to three'.
a. Slope
b. Slope of a line
c. -module
d. Ratio

33. In mathematics, the _____ is a numerical invariant of an ordered 4-tuple of distinct points on a line and of an ordered 4-tuple of concurrent lines in a plane. It had been defined in deep antiquity, possibly already by Euclid, and was considered by Pappus, who remarked its key invariance property. It was extensively studied in the 19th century.
a. Projective transformation
b. Projective space
c. Cross ratio
d. Cross-ratio

34. _____ projection is type of parallel projection technique, used to create a pictural drawing of an object by rotating the object on an axis relative to a projection, or picture plane.

There are three main types of _____ projection: isometric, dimetric, and trimetric projection.

'_____' means 'to measure along axes' Within orthographic projection, _____ projection shows an image of an object as viewed from a skew direction in order to reveal more than one side in the same picture, unlike other orthographic projections which show multiple views of the same object along different axes.

a. ADHM construction
b. Axonometric
c. AA postulate
d. ADE classification

35. In mathematics, an _____ is the finite or bounded case of a conic section, the geometric shape that results from cutting a circular conical or cylindrical surface with an oblique plane . It is also the locus of all points of the plane whose distances to two fixed points add to the same constant.

_____s also arise as images of a circle or a sphere under parallel projection, and some cases of perspective projection.

a. AA postulate
b. ADHM construction
c. ADE classification
d. Ellipse

36. In mathematics, a _____ is a number that can be expressed as an integral of an algebraic function over an algebraic domain. The concept has been promoted by Maxim Kontsevich and Don Zagier.

In elementary mathematics each group of three digits in a number is called a _____

a. -module
b. Bounded
c. 1-center problem
d. Period

37. In mathematics, a _____ section is a curve obtained by intersecting a cone (more precisely, a circular conical surface) with a plane. A _____ section is therefore a restriction of a quadric surface to the plane. The _____ sections were named and studied as long ago as 200 BC, when Apollonius of Perga undertook a systematic study of their properties.

a. -module
b. 1-center problem
c. Conic
d. 11-cell

Chapter 7. Projective Geometry

38. In geometry, the _____ line (or simply the _____) to a curve at a given point is the straight line that 'just touches' the curve at that point (in the sense explained more precisely below.) As it passes through the point of tangency, the _____ line is 'going in the same direction' as the curve, and in this sense it is the best straight-line approximation to the curve at that point. The same definition applies to space curves and curves in n-dimensional Euclidean space.

   a. Metric signature
   b. Measuring function
   c. Cartan connection
   d. Tangent

39. In differential geometry, _____ are, roughly, points that can almost be joined by a 1-parameter family of geodesics. For example, on a sphere, the north-pole and south-pole are connected by any meridian.

Suppose p and q are points on a Riemannian manifold, and >γ is a geodesic that connects p and q.

   a. Vector flow
   b. Space form
   c. Filling radius
   d. Conjugate points

40. In geometry, the terms _____ and polar are used to describe a point and a line that have a unique reciprocal relationship with respect to a given conic section. If the point lies on the conic section, its polar is the tangent line to the conic section at that point.

For a given circle, the operation of reciprocation in a circle corresponds to transforming each point in the plane into its polar line and each line in the plane into its _____.

   a. 11-cell
   b. Pole
   c. -module
   d. 1-center problem

41. In geometry, a _____ is a polygon with six edges and six vertices. A regular _____ has Schl>äfli symbol {6}.

The internal angles of a regular _____ are all 120>° and the _____ has 720 degrees T. It has 6 rotational symmetries and 6 reflection symmetries, making up the dihedral group D_6. The longest diagonals of a regular _____, connecting diametrically opposite vertices, are twice its sides in length.

a. Regular polygon
b. Hexadecagon
c. Right triangle
d. Hexagon

42. _____ , was a French mathematician, physicist, and religious philosopher. He was a child prodigy who was educated by his father, a civil servant. Pascal's earliest work was in the natural and applied sciences where he made important contributions to the construction of mechanical calculators, the study of fluids, and clarified the concepts of pressure and vacuum by generalizing the work of Evangelista Torricelli.
   a. 11-cell
   b. 1-center problem
   c. -module
   d. Blaise Pascal

43. A _____ is a six-pointed geometric star figure, {6/2} or 2{3}, the compound of two equilateral triangles. The intersection is a regular hexagon.
   a. Hexagram
   b. Right triangle
   c. Simple polygon
   d. Golygon

Chapter 8. Geometric Introduction to Topological Transformations

1. Topology includes many subfields. The most basic and traditional division within topology is point-set topology, which establishes the foundational aspects of topology and investigates concepts inherent to _____ spaces - basic examples being compactness and connectedness; algebraic topology, which generally tries to measure degrees of connectivity using algebraic constructs such as homotopy groups and homology; and geometric topology, which primarily studies manifolds and their embeddings (placements) in other manifolds. Some of the most active areas, such as low dimensional topology and graph theory, do not fit neatly in this division.
    a. 11-cell
    b. -module
    c. 1-center problem
    d. Topological

2. _____ is a major area of mathematics that has emerged through the development of concepts from geometry and set theory, such as those of space, dimension, shape, transformation and others.

    Ideas that are now classified as topological were expressed as early as 1736, and toward the end of the 19th century a distinct discipline developed, called in Latin the geometria situs or analysis situs , and later gaining the modern name of _____. In the middle of the 20th century, this was an important growth area within mathematics.

    a. Topological
    b. Metric space
    c. -module
    d. Topology

3. In mathematics, a _____ could be any function mapping a set X onto another set or onto itself. However, often the set X has some additional algebraic or geometric structure and the term '_____' refers to a function from X to itself which preserves this structure.

    Examples include linear _____s and affine _____s such as rotations, reflections and translations.

    a. -module
    b. 1-center problem
    c. Transformation
    d. Codomain

4. In the mathematical field of topology, a homeomorphism or topological isomorphism or _____ function = shape, form) is a continuous function between two topological spaces that has a continuous inverse function. Homeomorphisms are the isomorphisms in the category of topological spaces -- that is, they are the mappings which preserve all the topological properties of a given space. Two spaces with a homeomorphism between them are called homeomorphic, and from a topological viewpoint they are the same.

Chapter 8. Geometric Introduction to Topological Transformations

a. -module
b. 1-center problem
c. 11-cell
d. Bicontinuous

5. A function or map from one topological space to another is called _____ if the inverse image of any open set is open. If the function maps the real numbers to the real numbers (both spaces with the Standard Topology), then this definition of _____ is equivalent to the definition of _____ in calculus. If a _____ function is one-to-one and onto and if the inverse of the function is also _____, then the function is called a homeomorphism and the domain of the function is said to be homeomorphic to the range.

   a. Metric space
   b. Continuous
   c. Fresnel integrals
   d. -module

6. In the mathematical field of topology, a _____ or topological isomorphism is a bicontinuous function between two topological spaces. _____s are the isomorphisms in the category of topological spaces -- that is, they are the mappings which preserve all the topological properties of a given space. Two spaces with a _____ between them are called homeomorphic, and from a topological viewpoint they are the same.

Roughly speaking, a topological space is a geometric object, and the _____ is a continuous stretching and bending of the object into a new shape. Thus, a square and a circle are homeomorphic to each other, but a sphere and a donut are not.

   a. -module
   b. 11-cell
   c. 1-center problem
   d. Homeomorphism

7. A subset of a topological space X is a _____ if it is a connected space when viewed as a subspace of X.

One may perceive mathematical spaces which are not connected. For instance, the space resulting from the deletion of an infinite line from the plane is not connected for two points on opposite sides of the deleted line cannot be joined by a path within the space. Other examples of disconnected spaces (that is, spaces which are not connected) include the plane with an annulus removed, as well as the union of two disjoint disks in two-dimensional Euclidean space.

Chapter 8. Geometric Introduction to Topological Transformations

a. Boundary point
b. -module
c. 1-center problem
d. Connected set

8. In mathematical analysis and related areas of mathematics, a set is called _____, if it is, in a certain sense, of finite size. Conversely a set which is not _____ is called unbounded.

A set S of real numbers is called _____ from above if there is a real number k such that k >≥ s for all s in S. The number k is called an upper bound of S. The terms _____ from below and lower bound are similarly defined.

a. 11-cell
b. -module
c. 1-center problem
d. Bounded

9. A curve ☒> is said to be closed or a loop if ☒> and if ☒>. A _____ is thus a continuous mapping of the circle S^1; a simple _____ is also called a Jordan curve or a Jordan arc. The Jordan curve theorem states that such curves divide the plane into an 'interior' and an 'exterior'.

a. 1-center problem
b. -module
c. 11-cell
d. Closed curve

10. In mathematics, a _____ consists of the points through which a continuously moving point passes. This notion captures the intuitive idea of a geometrical one-dimensional object, which furthermore is connected in the sense of having no discontinuities or gaps. Simple examples include the sine wave as the basic _____ underlying simple harmonic motion, and the parabola.

a. Singular point
b. Sectrix of Maclaurin
c. Curve
d. Dual curve

Chapter 8. Geometric Introduction to Topological Transformations

11. As for binary digits, there are two variants of parity bits: _____ bit and odd parity bit. An _____ bit is set to 1 if the number of ones in a given set of bits is odd (making the total number of ones, including the parity bit, even.) An odd parity bit is set to 1 if the number of ones in a given set of bits is even (making the total number of ones, including the parity bit, odd.)

   a. Odd parity
   b. ADE classification
   c. AA postulate
   d. Even parity

12. In topology, the _____ states that every non-self-intersecting loop in the plane divides the plane into an 'inside' and an 'outside' region, and any path connecting a point of one region to a point of the other intersects that loop somewhere. It was proved by Oswald Veblen in 1905.

The precise mathematical statement is as follows.

Let c be a simple closed curve in the plane R^2. Then the complement of the image of c consists of two distinct connected components. One of these components is bounded (the interior) and the other is unbounded (the exterior). The image of c is the boundary of each component.

   a. 1-center problem
   b. 11-cell
   c. Jordan curve theorem
   d. -module

13. As for binary digits, there are two variants of parity bits: even parity bit and _____ bit. An even parity bit is set to 1 if the number of ones in a given set of bits is odd (making the total number of ones, including the parity bit, even.) An _____ bit is set to 1 if the number of ones in a given set of bits is even (making the total number of ones, including the parity bit, odd.)

   a. AA postulate
   b. ADE classification
   c. Odd parity
   d. Even parity

14. In formal mathematical logic, the concept of a _____ may be taken to mean a formula that can be derived according to the derivation rules of a fixed formal system. The statements of a theory as expressed in a formal language are called its elementary _____s and are said to be true.

The essential property of _____s is that they are derivable using a fixed set of inference rules and axioms without any additional assumptions.

Chapter 8. Geometric Introduction to Topological Transformations

a. Rule of inference
b. Logical axioms
c. Proof
d. Theorem

15. In mathematics, a _____ is a result saying that a function F will have at least one fixed point (a point x for which F(x) = x), under some conditions on F that can be stated in general terms. Results of this kind are amongst the most generally useful in mathematics.

The Banach _____ gives a general criterion guaranteeing that, if it is satisfied, the procedure of iterating a function yields a fixed point.

a. -module
b. 1-center problem
c. Fixed point theorem
d. 11-cell

16. In geometry, topology and related branches of mathematics a spatial _____ describes a specific object within a given space that consists of neither volume, area, length, nor any other higher dimensional analogue. Thus, a _____ is a 0-dimensional object. Because of their nature as one of the simplest geometric concepts, they are often used in one form or another as the fundamental constituents of geometry, physics, vector graphics, and many other fields.

a. 1-center problem
b. -module
c. Bounded
d. Point

17. In geometry, the terms _____ and polar are used to describe a point and a line that have a unique reciprocal relationship with respect to a given conic section. If the point lies on the conic section, its polar is the tangent line to the conic section at that point.

For a given circle, the operation of reciprocation in a circle corresponds to transforming each point in the plane into its polar line and each line in the plane into its _____.

a. 11-cell
b. -module
c. 1-center problem
d. Pole

Chapter 8. Geometric Introduction to Topological Transformations

18. In geometry, the _____ line (or simply the _____) to a curve at a given point is the straight line that 'just touches' the curve at that point (in the sense explained more precisely below.) As it passes through the point of tangency, the _____ line is 'going in the same direction' as the curve, and in this sense it is the best straight-line approximation to the curve at that point. The same definition applies to space curves and curves in n-dimensional Euclidean space.
    a. Cartan connection
    b. Tangent
    c. Metric signature
    d. Measuring function

19. In differential geometry, one can attach to every point x of a differentiable manifold a tangent space, a real vector space which intuitively contains the possible 'directions' in which one can pass through x. The elements of the tangent space are called _____ at x. This is a generalization of the notion of a bound vector in a Euclidean space.
    a. Tangent vectors
    b. -module
    c. 11-cell
    d. 1-center problem

20. In mathematics and computer science, _____ is the study of graphs: mathematical structures used to model pairwise relations between objects from a certain collection. A 'graph' in this context refers to a collection of vertices or 'nodes' and a collection of edges that connect pairs of vertices. A graph may be undirected, meaning that there is no distinction between the two vertices associated with each edge, or its edges may be directed from one vertex to another; see graph (mathematics) for more detailed definitions and for other variations in the types of graphs that are commonly considered.
    a. 11-cell
    b. Graph theory
    c. -module
    d. 1-center problem

21. In the geometry of curves a _____ is a point of where the first derivative of curvature is zero. This is typically a local maximum or minimum of curvature. Other special cases may occur, for instance when the second derivative is also zero, or when the curvature is constant.
    a. Non-Euclidean crystallographic group
    b. Holomorphic vector bundle
    c. Coordinate-induced basis
    d. Vertex

Chapter 8. Geometric Introduction to Topological Transformations

22. Graphs which allow the construction of so called Eulerian circuits are called _____. Euler observed that a necessary condition for the existence of Eulerian circuits is that all vertices in the graph have an even degree, and that for an Eulerian path either all, or all but two (i.e., the two endpoint) vertices have an even degree; this means the K>önigsberg graph is not Eulerian. Sometimes a graph that has an Eulerian path, but not an Eulerian circuit (in other words, it is an open path, and does not start and end at the same vertex) is called semi-Eulerian.
    a. ADHM construction
    b. Eulerian graphs
    c. AA postulate
    d. ADE classification

23. In technical applications of 3D computer graphics (CAx) such as computer-aided design and computer-aided manufacturing, _____s are one way of representing objects. The other ways are wireframe (lines and curves) and solids. Point clouds are also sometimes used as temporary ways to represent an object, with the goal of using the points to create one or more of the three permanent representations.
    a. Solid modeling
    b. Surface
    c. Geometric primitive
    d. Space partitioning

24. In mathematics, _____ is a branch of bifurcation theory in the study of dynamical systems; it is also a particular special case of more general singularity theory in geometry.

Bifurcation theory studies and classifies phenomena characterized by sudden shifts in behavior arising from small changes in circumstances, analysing how the qualitative nature of equation solutions depends on the parameters that appear in the equation. This may lead to sudden and dramatic changes, for example the unpredictable timing and magnitude of a landslide.

   a. Hopf bifurcation
   b. Catastrophe theory
   c. Pitchfork bifurcation
   d. Saddle-node bifurcation

25. In mathematics, the _____ is a certain non-orientable surface, i.e., a surface (a two-dimensional manifold) with no distinct 'inner' and 'outer' sides. Other related non-orientable objects include the M>öbius strip and the real projective plane. Whereas a M>öbius strip is a two dimensional surface with boundary, a _____ has no boundary.

Chapter 8. Geometric Introduction to Topological Transformations 85

   a. Klein bottle
   b. -module
   c. 11-cell
   d. 1-center problem

26. In mathematics, _____ is the area of topology that studies mathematical knots. While inspired by knots which appear in daily life in shoelaces and rope, a mathematician's knot differs in that the ends are joined together to prevent it from becoming undone. In precise mathematical language, a knot is an embedding of a circle in 3-dimensional Euclidean space, R^3.
   a. -module
   b. 11-cell
   c. 1-center problem
   d. Knot theory

27. A _____ is often defined as a geometric object with flat faces and straight edges .

This definition of a _____ is not very precise, and to a modern mathematician is quite unsatisfactory. Grünbaum observed that:

The Original Sin in the theory of polyhedra goes back to Euclid, and through Kepler, Poinsot, Cauchy and many others ...

   a. 1-center problem
   b. Polyhedra
   c. -module
   d. Polyhedron

28. In geometry an _____ is a highly symmetric, semi-regular convex polyhedron composed of two or more types of regular polygons meeting in identical vertices. They are distinct from the Platonic solids, which are composed of only one type of polygon meeting in identical vertices, and from the Johnson solids, whose regular polygonal faces do not meet in identical vertices. The symmetry of the _____s excludes the members of the dihedral group, the prisms and antiprisms.
   a. AA postulate
   b. Icosidodecahedron
   c. ADE classification
   d. Archimedean solid

Chapter 8. Geometric Introduction to Topological Transformations

29. In mathematics, and more specifically in algebraic topology and polyhedral combinatorics, the _____ is a topological invariant, a number that describes a topological space's shape or structure regardless of the way it is bent. It is commonly denoted by χ (>χ '>chi).

The _____ was originally defined for polyhedra and used to prove various theorems about them, including the classification of the Platonic solids.

   a. Alexander duality
   b. Essential manifold
   c. Abstract polytope
   d. Euler characteristic

30. A _____ is a visual representation of an area--a symbolic depiction highlighting relationships between elements of that space such as objects, regions, and themes.

Many _____s are static two-dimensional, geometrically accurate (or approximately accurate) representations of three-dimensional space, while others are dynamic or interactive, even three-dimensional. Although most commonly used to depict geography, _____s may represent any space, real or imagined, without regard to context or scale; e.g. Brain mapping, DNA mapping, and extraterrestrial mapping.

   a. 1-center problem
   b. -module
   c. Map
   d. 11-cell

31. In mathematics, the _____ states that given any separation of a plane into contiguous regions, called a map, the regions can be colored using at most four colors so that no two adjacent regions have the same color. Two regions are called adjacent only if they share a border segment, not just a point.

Three colors are adequate for simpler maps, but an additional fourth color is required for some maps, such as a map in which one region is surrounded by an odd number of other regions that touch each other in a cycle.

   a. 11-cell
   b. -module
   c. 1-center problem
   d. Four color theorem

Chapter 9. Non-Euclidean Geometries

1. In mathematics, _____ geometry describes hyperbolic and elliptic geometry, which are contrasted with Euclidean geometry. The essential difference between Euclidean and _____ geometry is the nature of parallel lines. Euclid's fifth postulate, the parallel postulate, is equivalent to Playfair's postulate, which states that, within a two-dimensional plane, for any given line l and a point A, which is not on l, there is exactly one line through A that does not intersect l.
   a. Non-Euclidean
   b. Codimension
   c. Coplanar
   d. Coaxial

2. A non-Euclidean geometry is characterized by a non-vanishing Riemann curvature tensor. Examples of _____ include the hyperbolic and elliptic geometry, which are contrasted with a Euclidean geometry. The essential difference between Euclidean and non-Euclidean geometry is the nature of parallel lines.
   a. 11-cell
   b. 1-center problem
   c. -module
   d. Non-Euclidean geometries

3. _____ is a geometry based on an axiom system that does not assume the parallel postulate or any of its alternatives. The term was introduced by J>ános Bolyai in 1832. It is sometimes referred to as neutral geometry, as it is neutral with respect to the parallel postulate.
   a. Adjacent angles
   b. AA postulate
   c. Elliptic geometry
   d. Absolute geometry

4. In the field of mathematical logic, a clear distinction is made between two notions of _____s: logical _____s and non-logical _____s (somewhat similar to the ancient distinction between '_____s' and 'postulates' respectively)

These are certain formulas in a formal language that are universally valid, that is, formulas that are satisfied by every assignment of values. Usually one takes as logical _____s at least some minimal set of tautologies that is sufficient for proving all tautologies in the language; in the case of predicate logic more logical _____s than that are required, in order to prove logical truths that are not tautologies in the strict sense.

Chapter 9. Non-Euclidean Geometries

In propositional logic it is common to take as logical _____s all formulae of the following forms, where φ, χ, and ψ can be any formulae of the language and where the included primitive connectives are only '¬' for negation of the immediately following proposition and '→' for implication from antecedent to consequent propositions:

1. $\phi \to (\psi \to \phi)$
2. $(\phi \to (\psi \to \chi)) \to ((\phi \to \psi) \to (\phi \to \chi))$
3. $(\neg\phi \to \neg\psi) \to (\psi \to \phi)$.

Each of these patterns is an _____ schema, a rule for generating an infinite number of _____s. For example, if A, B, and C are propositional variables, then $A \to (B \to A)$ and $(A \to \neg B) \to (C \to (A \to \neg B))$ are both instances of _____ schema 1, and hence are _____s.

a. Inductive reasoning
b. AA postulate
c. ADE classification
d. Axiom

5. In the field of mathematical logic, a clear distinction is made between two notions of axioms: _____ and non-_____

These are certain formulas in a formal language that are universally valid, that is, formulas that are satisfied by every assignment of values. Usually one takes as _____ at least some minimal set of tautologies that is sufficient for proving all tautologies in the language; in the case of predicate logic more _____ than that are required, in order to prove logical truths that are not tautologies in the strict sense.

In propositional logic it is common to take as _____ all formulae of the following forms, where φ, χ, and ψ can be any formulae of the language and where the included primitive connectives are only '¬' for negation of the immediately following proposition and '→' for implication from antecedent to consequent propositions:

1. $\phi \to (\psi \to \phi)$
2. $(\phi \to (\psi \to \chi)) \to ((\phi \to \psi) \to (\phi \to \chi))$
3. $(\neg\phi \to \neg\psi) \to (\psi \to \phi)$.

Each of these patterns is an axiom schema, a rule for generating an infinite number of axioms. For example, if A, B, and C are propositional variables, then $A \to (B \to A)$ and $(A \to \neg B) \to (C \to (A \to \neg B))$ are both instances of axiom schema 1, and hence are axioms.

Chapter 9. Non-Euclidean Geometries 89

   a. Logically equivalent
   b. Theorem
   c. Contrapositive
   d. Logical axioms

6. In mathematics, an _____ is the finite or bounded case of a conic section, the geometric shape that results from cutting a circular conical or cylindrical surface with an oblique plane . It is also the locus of all points of the plane whose distances to two fixed points add to the same constant.

_____s also arise as images of a circle or a sphere under parallel projection, and some cases of perspective projection.

   a. ADE classification
   b. Ellipse
   c. ADHM construction
   d. AA postulate

7. In mathematics, _____ is a non-Euclidean geometry, meaning that the parallel postulate of Euclidean geometry is replaced. The parallel postulate in Euclidean geometry is equivalent to the statement that, in two dimensional space, for any given line l and point P not on l, there is exactly one line through P that does not intersect l; i.e., that is parallel to l. In _____ there are at least two distinct lines through P which do not intersect l, so the parallel postulate is false.
   a. Margulis lemma
   b. Complex geodesic
   c. Tameness conjecture
   d. Hyperbolic geometry

8. In geometry and trigonometry, an _____ is the figure formed by two rays sharing a common endpoint, called the vertex of the _____ . The magnitude of the _____ is the 'amount of rotation' that separates the two rays, and can be measured by considering the length of circular arc swept out when one ray is rotated about the vertex to coincide with the other Where there is no possibility of confusion, the term '_____' is used interchangeably for both the geometric configuration itself and for its angular magnitude (which is simply a numerical quantity.)
   a. ADHM construction
   b. ADE classification
   c. AA postulate
   d. Angle

9. Left-handedness is the preference for the left hand over the right for everyday activities such as writing. Most _____ people exhibit some degree of ambidexterity. Left-handedness is relatively uncommon; 90 to 93 percent of the adult population is right-handed.

   a. 11-cell
   b. -module
   c. 1-center problem
   d. Left-handed

10. A _____ of a curve is the envelope of a family of congruent circles centered on the curve. It generalises the concept of _____ lines.

It is sometimes called the offset curve but the term 'offset' often refers also to translation.

   a. Cissoid
   b. Cassini oval
   c. Trisectrix of Maclaurin
   d. Parallel

11. Right-handedness is the form of handedness in which one has greater coordination and dexterity in the right hand than in the left hand. _____ individuals will perform everyday tasks such as writing, cooking and carrying out one's personal hygiene with the right hand.

A variety of studies suggest that 70% to 90% of the world population are _____ rather than left-handed or any other form of handedness.

   a. Right-handed
   b. -module
   c. 11-cell
   d. 1-center problem

12. A _____ is one of the basic shapes of geometry: a polygon with three corners or vertices and three sides or edges which are line segments. A _____ with vertices A, B, and C is denoted ABC.

In Euclidean geometry any three non-collinear points determine a unique _____ and a unique plane (i.e. a two-dimensional Euclidean space.)

Chapter 9. Non-Euclidean Geometries 91

a. Brocard point
b. -module
c. 1-center problem
d. Triangle

13. In geometry, topology and related branches of mathematics a spatial _____ describes a specific object within a given space that consists of neither volume, area, length, nor any other higher dimensional analogue. Thus, a _____ is a 0-dimensional object. Because of their nature as one of the simplest geometric concepts, they are often used in one form or another as the fundamental constituents of geometry, physics, vector graphics, and many other fields.
   a. -module
   b. Bounded
   c. 1-center problem
   d. Point

14. In geometry, two sets of points are called _____ if one can be transformed into the other by an isometry, i.e., a combination of translations, rotations and reflections. Less formally, two figures are _____ if they have the same shape and size, but are in different positions (for instance one may be rotated, flipped, or simply placed somewhere else).
   a. 1-center problem
   b. Bounded
   c. -module
   d. Congruent

15. In geometry, a _____ is a polygon with four 'sides' or edges and four vertices or corners. Sometimes, the term quadrangle is used, for analogy with triangle, and sometimes tetragon for consistency with pentagon (5-sided), hexagon (6-sided) and so on. The word _____ is made of the words quad and lateral.
   a. 11-cell
   b. 1-center problem
   c. -module
   d. Quadrilateral

16. A _____ is a quadrilateral with two equal sides perpendicular to the base. It is named after Giovanni Gerolamo Saccheri, who used it extensively in his book Euclid vindicatus (1733), an attempt to prove the parallel postulate. Since the _____ was first considered by Omar Khayyam in the late 11th century, the quadrilateral has alternatively been named the Khayyam-_____.

Chapter 9. Non-Euclidean Geometries

a. Margulis lemma
b. Saccheri quadrilateral
c. Hyperbolic triangle
d. Tameness conjecture

17. In mathematics, a binary relation R over a set X is _____ if whenever an element a is related to an element b, and b is in turn related to an element c, then a is also related to c.

Transitivity is a key property of both partial order relations and equivalence relations.

For example, 'is greater than,' 'is at least as great as,' and 'is equal to' (equality) are _____ relations:

whenever A > B and B > C, then also A > C
whenever A >≥ B and B >≥ C, then also A >≥ C
whenever A = B and B = C, then also A = C

For some time, economists and philosophers believed that preference was a _____ relation; however, there are now mathematical theories which demonstrate that preferences and other significant economic results can be modelled without resorting to this assumption.

a. 11-cell
b. 1-center problem
c. -module
d. Transitive

18. A _____ is a hyperbolic quadrilateral. It has a base, AB, two legs standing at right angles to it, AC and BD, and the summit, CD, meets one of the two legs at a right angle and the other leg at a non-obtuse angle. .
a. Lambert quadrilateral
b. Tameness conjecture
c. Hyperbolic geometry
d. Gyrovectors

19. In mathematics and solid state physics, the first _____ is a uniquely defined primitive cell of the reciprocal lattice. It is found by the same method as for the Wigner-Seitz cell in the Bravais lattice. The importance of the _____ stems from the Bloch wave description of waves in a periodic medium, in which it is found that the solutions can be completely characterized by their behavior in a single _____.

Chapter 9. Non-Euclidean Geometries

a. -module
b. 11-cell
c. 1-center problem
d. Brillouin zone

20. In mathematics, a (B, N) _____ is a structure on groups of Lie type that allows one to give uniform proofs of many results, instead of giving a large number of case-by-case proofs. Roughly speaking, it shows that all such groups are similar to the general linear group over a field. They were invented by the mathematician Jacques Tits, and are also sometimes known as Tits systems.
    a. Dihedral group
    b. Hanna Neumann conjecture
    c. Pair
    d. Free group

21. In a totally ordered set all elements are mutually comparable, so such a set can have at most one minimal element and at most one maximal element. Then, due to mutual comparability, the minimal element will also be the least element and the maximal element will also be the greatest element. Thus in a totally ordered set we can simply use the terms minimum and _____.
    a. Maximum
    b. -module
    c. Hyperbolic angle
    d. Fresnel integrals

22. In geometry, the _____ of a vertex of a polyhedron is the amount by which the sum of the angles of the faces at the vertex falls short of a full circle. If the sum of the angles exceeds a full circle, as occurs in some vertices of most (not all) non-convex polyhedra, then the _____ is negative. If a polyhedron is convex, then the _____s of all of its vertices are positive.
    a. Spherical polyhedron
    b. Defect
    c. Pyritohedron
    d. Parallelepiped

23. In mathematics, a _____ consists of the points through which a continuously moving point passes. This notion captures the intuitive idea of a geometrical one-dimensional object, which furthermore is connected in the sense of having no discontinuities or gaps. Simple examples include the sine wave as the basic _____ underlying simple harmonic motion, and the parabola.

a. Singular point
b. Dual curve
c. Sectrix of Maclaurin
d. Curve

24. In hyperbolic geometry, a _____, hypercircle or equidistant curve is a curve whose points have the same orthogonal distance from a given straight line.

Given a straight line L and a point P not on L, we can construct a _____ by taking all points Q on the same side of L as P, with perpendicular distance to L equal to that of P.

The line L is called the axis, center, or base line of the _____.

a. Fuchsian group
b. Hypercycle
c. Horocycle
d. Horoball

25. In mathematics, two vectors are _____ if they are perpendicular, i.e., they form a right angle. The word comes from the Greek >á½€>ρ>θϊŒ>ς , meaning 'straight', and >>γ>ω>vĪ >α (gonia), meaning 'angle'. For example, a subway and the street above, although they do not physically intersect, are _____ if they cross at a right angle.
a. Orthogonal
b. Embedding
c. Algebraic K-theory
d. Interior algebra

26. In mathematics, _____ are a family of curves in the plane that intersect a given family of curves at right angles. The problem is classical, but is now understood by means of complex analysis; see for example harmonic conjugate.

For a family of level curves described by g(x,y) = C, where C is a constant, the _____ may be found as the level curves of a new function f(x,y) by solving the partial differential equation

$$\nabla f \cdot \nabla g = 0$$

for f(x,y).

a. Axis-aligned object
b. Edge
c. Orthogonal trajectories
d. Ambient space

27. A _____ is the path a moving object follows through space. The object might be a projectile or a satellite, for example. It thus includes the meaning of orbit - the path of a planet, an asteroid or a comet as it travels around a central mass.
a. 1-center problem
b. -module
c. 11-cell
d. Trajectory

28. _____ is a non-Euclidean geometry, in which, given a line L and a point p outside L, there exists no line parallel to L passing through p. _____, like hyperbolic geometry, violates Euclid's parallel postulate, which can be interpreted as asserting that there is exactly one line parallel to L passing through p. In _____, there are no parallel lines at all.
a. Adjacent angles
b. Absolute geometry
c. AA postulate
d. Elliptic geometry

29. In mathematics, a _____ could be any function mapping a set X onto another set or onto itself. However, often the set X has some additional algebraic or geometric structure and the term '_____' refers to a function from X to itself which preserves this structure.

Examples include linear _____s and affine _____s such as rotations, reflections and translations.

a. Codomain
b. -module
c. 1-center problem
d. Transformation

30. In geometry, a _____ is a degenerate polygon with two sides (edges) and two vertices.

A _____ must be regular because its two edges are the same length. It has Schl>äfli symbol {2}.

In Euclidean geometry a _____ is always degenerate. However, in spherical geometry a nondegenerate _____ can exist if the vertices are antipodal. The internal angle of the spherical _____ vertex can be any angle between 0 and 180 degrees. Such a spherical polygon can also be called a lune.

a. -module
b. 1-center problem
c. 11-cell
d. Digon

31. A _____ proof is a mathematical proof that a particular theory is consistent. The early development of mathematical proof theory was driven by the desire to provide finitary _____ proofs for all of mathematics as part of Hilbert's program. Hilbert's program was strongly impacted by incompleteness theorems, which showed that sufficiently strong proof theories cannot prove their own _____

a. 1-center problem
b. Consistency
c. Valid argument
d. -module

32. In geometry, the Cayley-_____ Klein disk model, and the Beltrami-_____, is a model of n-dimensional hyperbolic geometry in which points are represented by the points in the interior of the n-dimensional unit ball and lines are represented by the chords, straight line segments with endpoints on the boundary sphere. It made its first appearance in two memoirs of Eugenio Beltrami published in 1868, first for n=2 and then for general n, devoted to showing equiconsistency of hyperbolic geometry with ordinary Euclidean geometry.

The formula for the distance was first written down by Arthur Cayley in the context of projective and spherical geometry.

a. 1-center problem
b. -module
c. 11-cell
d. Klein model

33. In chemistry, the _____ molecular geometry describes the arrangement of three or more atoms placed at an expected bond angle of 180Â°. _____ organic molecules, e.g. acetylene, are often described by invoking sp orbital hybridization for the carbon centers. Many _____ molecules exist, prominent examples include CO_2, HCN, and xenon difluoride.

Chapter 9. Non-Euclidean Geometries 97

  a. -module
  b. 1-center problem
  c. 11-cell
  d. Linear

34. A _____ is a basic structure in incidence geometry.

_____s can be seen as a generalization of 2 >− (v,k,1) designs, where the requirement that every block contains the same number of points is dropped and the essential structural characteristic is that 2 points are incident with exactly 1 line. The term _____ was coined by Libois in 1964, though many results about _____s are much older.

  a. Facet
  b. Noncommutative geometry
  c. Fredholm module
  d. Linear space

35. In mathematics, a _____ or distance function is a function which defines a distance between elements of a set. A set with a _____ is called a _____ space. A _____ induces a topology on a set but not all topologies can be generated by a _____.

  a. Comparison triangle
  b. Metric
  c. Polyhedral space
  d. Systolic inequalities for curves on surfaces

36. _____ is the boundless, three-dimensional extent in which objects and events occur and have relative position and direction. Physical _____ is often conceived in three linear dimensions, although modern physicists usually consider it, with time, to be part of the boundless four-dimensional continuum known as spacetime. In mathematics _____s with different numbers of dimensions and with different underlying structures can be examined.

  a. 11-cell
  b. 1-center problem
  c. -module
  d. Space

37. In mathematics, the _____ is an extended non-negative real number associated to any metric space. The _____ generalizes the notion of the dimension of a real vector space. In particular, the _____ of a single point is zero, the _____ of a line is one, the _____ of the plane is two, etc.

Chapter 9. Non-Euclidean Geometries

a. Multibrot set
b. Hausdorff dimension
c. Gravity set
d. Dedekind eta function

38. _____, considered by Hermann Minkowski in the 19th century, is a form of geometry in which the usual metric of Euclidean geometry is replaced by a new metric in which the distance between two points is the sum of the (absolute) differences of their coordinates. The taxicab metric is also known as rectilinear distance, L_1 distance or L^1 norm , city block distance, Manhattan distance, or Manhattan length, with corresponding variations in the name of the geometry. The last name alludes to the grid layout of most streets on the island of Manhattan, which causes the shortest path a car could take between two points in the city to have length equal to the points' distance in _____.
a. Taxicab geometry
b. Digital topology
c. Pruning
d. Grid cell topology

39. In mathematics, the _____ of a vector space V is the cardinality (i.e. the number of vectors) of a basis of V. It is sometimes called Hamel _____ or algebraic _____ to distinguish it from other types of _____. All bases of a vector space have equal cardinality and so the _____ of a vector space is uniquely defined. The _____ of the vector space V over the field F can be written as $\dim_F(V)$ or as [V : F], read '_____ of V over F'.
a. -module
b. 1-center problem
c. 11-cell
d. Dimension

40. In computer science, _____s, conditional expressions and conditional constructs are features of a programming language which perform different computations or actions depending on whether a programmer-specified condition evaluates to true or false Apart from the case of branch predication, this is always achieved by selectively altering the control flow based on some condition.

In imperative programming languages, the term '_____' is usually used, whereas in functional programming, the terms 'conditional expression' or 'conditional construct' are preferred, because these terms all have distinct meanings.

a. -module
b. 11-cell
c. Conditional statement
d. 1-center problem

Chapter 9. Non-Euclidean Geometries

41. A _____ is a mathematical table used in logic--specifically in connection with Boolean algebra, boolean functions, and propositional calculus--to compute the functional values of logical expressions on each of their functional arguments, that is, on each combination of values taken by their logical variables (Enderton 2001.) In particular, _____s can be used to tell whether a propositional expression is true for all legitimate input values, that is, logically valid.

 a. 11-cell
 b. 1-center problem
 c. Truth table
 d. -module

42. In logic and mathematics, _____ is an operation on propositions. For example, in classical logic _____ is normally interpreted by the truth function that takes truth to falsity and vice versa. In intuitionistic logic, according to the Brouwer-Heyting-Kolmogorov interpretation, the _____ of a proposition P is the proposition whose proofs are the refutations of P.

 a. 11-cell
 b. 1-center problem
 c. -module
 d. Negation

43. The term Validity in logic applies to arguments or statements.

An argument is valid if and only if the truth of its premises entails the truth of its conclusion, it would be self-contradictory to affirm the premises and deny the conclusion. The corresponding conditional of a _____ is a logical truth and the negation of its corresponding conditional is a contradiction.

 a. Consistency
 b. 1-center problem
 c. -module
 d. Valid argument

44. A _____ is a simple shape of Euclidean geometry consisting of those points in a plane which are the same distance from a given point called the centre. The common distance of the points of a _____ from its center is called its radius.

_____s are simple closed curves which divide the plane into two regions, an interior and an exterior.

a. Circle
b. Circumcircle
c. Gergonne point
d. Circumscribed circle

45. In geometry, a polygon can be either _____ or concave.

A _____ polygon is a simple polygon whose interior is a _____ set. The following properties of a simple polygon are all equivalent to convexity:

- Every internal angle is less than 180 degrees.
- Every line segment between two vertices remains inside or on the boundary of the polygon.

A simple polygon is strictly _____ if every internal angle is strictly less than 180 degrees. Equivalently, a polygon is strictly _____ if every line segment between two nonadjacent vertices of the polygon is strictly interior to the polygon except at its endpoints.

a. Separating axis theorem
b. Convex combination
c. Supporting hyperplane
d. Convex

46. In geometry, a _____ is any polygon with ten sides and ten angles, and usually refers to a regular _____, having all sides of equal length and all internal angles equal to 4>π/5 (144>°.) Its Schl>äfli symbol is {10}. The area of a regular _____ of side length a is given by

A regular _____ is constructible with a compass and straightedge.

a. Hendecagon
b. Dodecagon
c. Net
d. Decagon

47. In geometry, an _____ polygon is a polygon which has all sides of the same length.

Chapter 9. Non-Euclidean Geometries

For instance, an _____ triangle is a triangle of equal edge lengths. All _____ triangles are similar to each other, and have 60 degree internal angles.

a. Enneagram
b. Octadecagon
c. Octagon
d. Equilateral

48. In geometry, an _____ is a triangle in which all three sides are equal. In traditional or Euclidean geometry, _____s are also equiangular; that is, all three internal angles are also congruent to each other and are each 60°. They are regular polygons, and can therefore also be referred to as regular triangles.
    a. Orthocenter
    b. ADE classification
    c. Equilateral triangle
    d. AA postulate

49. In geometry, a _____ is a polygon with six edges and six vertices. A regular _____ has Schl>äfli symbol {6}.

The internal angles of a regular _____ are all 120>° and the _____ has 720 degrees T. It has 6 rotational symmetries and 6 reflection symmetries, making up the dihedral group D_6. The longest diagonals of a regular _____, connecting diametrically opposite vertices, are twice its sides in length.

a. Hexadecagon
b. Right triangle
c. Regular polygon
d. Hexagon

50. In geometry, an _____ is a polygon that has eight sides. A regular _____ is represented by the Schläfli symbol {8}. A regular _____ is constructible with compass and straightedge.
    a. Isothetic polygon
    b. Octadecagon
    c. Enneadecagon
    d. Octagon

51. In geometry, a _____ is any five-sided polygon. A _____ may be simple or self-intersecting. The internal angles in a simple _____ total 540°.

a. Right triangle
b. Pentagon
c. Five-pointed star
d. Simple polygon

52. In geometry a _____ is traditionally a plane figure that is bounded by a closed path or circuit, composed of a finite sequence of straight line segments (i.e., by a closed polygonal chain.) These segments are called its edges or sides, and the points where two edges meet are the _____'s vertices or corners. The interior of the _____ is sometimes called its body.
    a. Hexagram
    b. Dodecagon
    c. Polygon
    d. Right triangle

53. Use of _____ in Real-time imagery. The imaging system calls up the structure of _____ needed for the scene to be created from the database. This is transferred to active memory and finally, to the display system (screen, TV monitors etc) so that the scene can be viewed.
    a. 11-cell
    b. Polygons
    c. -module
    d. 1-center problem

54. In Euclidean geometry, a _____ is a quadrilateral with four right angles.Equivalently, it is an equiangular quadrilateral, but it is not necessarily equilateral.

A _____ with vertices ABCD would be denoted as ABCD.

- All angles are 90 degrees.
- Opposite sides are equal in length.
- Opposite sides are parallel.
- Diagonals are equal in length and bisect each other.

The formula for the perimeter of a _____.

If a _____ has length l and width w

- it has area A = lw
- perimeter P = 2l + 2w = 2(l + w)
- and each diagonal has length $\sqrt{l^2 + w^2}$.

When the length is equal to the width, the _____ is a square.

a. 11-cell
b. 1-center problem
c. -module
d. Rectangle

55. A _____ is a triangle in which one angle is a right angle.

The side opposite the right angle is called the hypotenuse (side [BC] in the figure below.) In addition, the sides adjacent to the right angle are called legs or catheti (singular: cathetus.)

a. Right triangle
b. Polygonal chain
c. Stellation
d. Simple polygon

56. In Euclidean geometry, a _____ is a regular quadrilateral. This means that it has four equal sides and four equal angles (90 degree angles, or right angles.) A _____ with vertices ABCD would be denoted ABCD.

a. Bounded
b. -module
c. 1-center problem
d. Square

57. In common usage, a cylinder is taken to mean a finite section of a right _____ with its ends closed to form two circular surfaces, as in the figure (right.) If the cylinder has a radius r and length (height) h, then its volume is given by

[×]>

and its surface area is:

- the area of the top +
- the area of the bottom +
- the area of the side .

Therefore without the top or bottom (lateral area), the surface area is

With the top and bottom, the surface area is

For a given volume, the cylinder with the smallest surface area has h = 2r. For a given surface area, the cylinder with the largest volume has h = 2r, i.e. the cylinder fits in a cube (height = diameter.)

Having a right _____ with a height h units and a base of radius r units with the coordinate axes chosen so that the origin is at the center of one base and the height is measured along the positive x-axis.

a. 11-cell
b. 1-center problem
c. Circular cylinder
d. -module

58. In linear algebra, a (linear) _____ is a subset of a vector space that is closed under multiplication by positive scalars. In other words, a subset C of a real vector space V is a _____ if and only if >λx belongs to C for any x in C and any positive scalar >λ of V (or, more succintly, if and only if >λC = C for any positive scalar >λ.)

A _____ is said to be pointed if it includes the null vector (origin) 0; otherwise it is said to be blunt.

a. Centerpoint
b. Complex line
c. Prismatic surface
d. Cone

Chapter 9. Non-Euclidean Geometries

59. In geometry, a _____ is a quadrilateral with two sets of parallel sides. The opposite or facing sides of a _____ are of equal length, and the opposite angles of a _____ are of equal size. The three-dimensional counterpart of a _____ is a parallelepiped.
    a. 11-cell
    b. 1-center problem
    c. Parallelogram
    d. -module

60. A polyhedron (plural _____ or polyhedrons) is often defined as a geometric solid with flat faces and straight edges .

This definition of a polyhedron is not very precise, and to a modern mathematician is quite unsatisfactory. Gr>ünbaum observed, 'The Original Sin in the theory of _____ goes back to Euclid, and through Kepler, Poinsot, Cauchy and many others ...

   a. Polyhedra
   b. 11-cell
   c. -module
   d. 1-center problem

61. In geometry, an n-sided _____ is a polyhedron made of an n-sided polygonal base, a translated copy, and n faces joining corresponding sides. Thus these joining faces are parallelograms. All cross-sections parallel to the base faces are the same.
    a. Hoberman sphere
    b. Hill tetrahedron
    c. Defect
    d. Prism

62. A _____ is a building where the outer surfaces are triangular and converge at a point. The base of a _____ is usually trilateral or quadrilateral (but may be of any polygon shape), meaning that a _____ usually has four or five faces. A _____'s design, with the majority of the weight closer to the ground, means that less material higher up on the _____ will be pushing down from above: this allowed early civilizations to create stable monumental structures.
    a. Pyramid
    b. 1-center problem
    c. -module
    d. 11-cell

63.

Chapter 9. Non-Euclidean Geometries

Every _____ has two diagonals connecting opposite pairs of vertices. Using congruent triangles, one can prove that the _____ is symmetric across each of these diagonals. It follows that any _____ has the following two properties:

1. Opposite angles of a _____ have equal measure.
2. The two diagonals of a _____ are perpendicular.

a. -module
b. 11-cell
c. 1-center problem
d. Rhombus

64. In solid geometry, _____ are two lines that do not intersect but are not parallel. Equivalently, they are lines that are not both in the same plane. A simple example of a pair of _____ is the pair of lines through opposite edges of a regular tetrahedron (or other non-degenerate tetrahedron.)
a. Semicircle
b. Line
c. Skew lines
d. Complementary angles

65. In every _____ there is a cuboid with all vertices tangent to the surface of said _____. It immediately becomes apparent that the cuboid inscribed in the _____ must be a cube with all vertices tangent to the surface of the _____.

Formula 1, shown below, finds the length of one side of the inscribed cube, and Formula 2 finds the volume of the inscribed cube.

a. Cone
b. Circumference
c. Point group in two dimensions
d. Sphere

66. In geometry, a figure with one pair of parallel sides is referred to as _____ in American English, and as a trapezium in British English. A _____ with vertices ABCD is denoted ABCD.

In North America, the term trapezium is used to refer to a quadrilateral with no parallel sides.

a. Rhomboid
b. -module
c. Trapezoid
d. Tangential quadrilateral

67. In the geometry of curves a _____ is a point of where the first derivative of curvature is zero. This is typically a local maximum or minimum of curvature. Other special cases may occur, for instance when the second derivative is also zero, or when the curvature is constant.

a. Holomorphic vector bundle
b. Non-Euclidean crystallographic group
c. Coordinate-induced basis
d. Vertex

68. A _____ is one of the most curvilinear basic geometric shapes:It has two faces, zero vertices, and zero edges. The surface formed by the points at a fixed distance from a given straight line, the axis of the _____. The solid enclosed by this surface and by two planes perpendicular to the axis is also called a _____.

a. -module
b. Bounded
c. 1-center problem
d. Cylinder

69. In mathematics, the _____ or Pythagoras' theorem is a relation in Euclidean geometry among the three sides of a right triangle. The theorem is usually written as an equation:

$$a^2 + b^2 = c^2$$

where c represents the length of the hypotenuse, and a and b represent the lengths of the other two sides. In words:

The square of the hypotenuse of a right triangle is equal to the sum of the squares on the other two sides.

a. Pythagorean theorem
b. 11-cell
c. 1-center problem
d. -module

Chapter 9. Non-Euclidean Geometries

70. In formal mathematical logic, the concept of a _____ may be taken to mean a formula that can be derived according to the derivation rules of a fixed formal system. The statements of a theory as expressed in a formal language are called its elementary _____s and are said to be true.

The essential property of _____s is that they are derivable using a fixed set of inference rules and axioms without any additional assumptions.

   a. Rule of inference
   b. Proof
   c. Logical axioms
   d. Theorem

71. In geometry, the notion of a _____ makes precise the idea of transporting data along a curve or family of curves in a parallel and consistent manner. There are a variety of kinds of _____s in modern geometry, depending on what sort of data one wants to transport. For instance, an affine _____, the most elementary type of _____, gives a means for transporting tangent vectors to a manifold from one point to another along a curve.

   a. Finsler manifold
   b. Covariant derivative
   c. Caustic
   d. Connection

ANSWER KEY

Chapter 1
1. a	2. d	3. d	4. c	5. d	6. b	7. d	8. d	9. d	10. d
11. b	12. c	13. b	14. d	15. d	16. b	17. a	18. d	19. a	20. d
21. a	22. d	23. a	24. d	25. d	26. c	27. a	28. c	29. a	30. b
31. d	32. a	33. c	34. d	35. c	36. c				

Chapter 2
1. d	2. d	3. d	4. b	5. d	6. c	7. d	8. c	9. d	10. c
11. d	12. c	13. d	14. d	15. c	16. c	17. d	18. d	19. a	20. c
21. c	22. b	23. b	24. d	25. c	26. d	27. b	28. b	29. d	30. a
31. d	32. b	33. a	34. d	35. d	36. d	37. d	38. d	39. c	40. d
41. c	42. b	43. d	44. c	45. d					

Chapter 3
1. c	2. c	3. b	4. c	5. a	6. d	7. a	8. a	9. d	10. b
11. b	12. d	13. d	14. a	15. d	16. d	17. d	18. d	19. d	20. d
21. b	22. d	23. a	24. d	25. a	26. d	27. d	28. a	29. c	30. c

Chapter 4
1. d	2. d	3. d	4. d	5. d	6. b	7. d	8. b	9. b	10. d
11. d	12. a	13. d	14. a	15. b	16. d	17. d	18. c	19. b	20. a
21. d	22. d	23. d	24. d	25. d	26. d	27. c	28. d	29. b	30. b
31. c	32. d	33. d	34. d	35. a	36. d	37. b	38. c	39. d	40. b
41. d	42. a	43. a	44. b	45. a	46. b				

Chapter 5
1. d	2. b	3. d	4. c	5. a	6. d	7. d	8. c	9. a	10. d
11. d	12. b	13. a	14. d	15. a	16. a	17. d	18. c	19. b	

Chapter 6
1. c	2. d	3. c	4. c	5. d	6. d	7. d	8. d	9. d	10. d
11. b	12. d	13. a	14. d	15. a	16. d	17. b			

Chapter 7
1. d	2. a	3. d	4. d	5. d	6. d	7. d	8. d	9. c	10. d
11. b	12. d	13. d	14. d	15. a	16. d	17. b	18. d	19. d	20. d
21. d	22. d	23. d	24. d	25. a	26. b	27. d	28. d	29. a	30. b
31. b	32. d	33. d	34. b	35. d	36. d	37. c	38. d	39. d	40. b
41. d	42. d	43. a							

Chapter 8
1. d	2. d	3. c	4. d	5. b	6. d	7. d	8. d	9. d	10. c
11. d	12. c	13. c	14. d	15. c	16. d	17. d	18. b	19. a	20. b
21. d	22. b	23. b	24. b	25. a	26. d	27. d	28. d	29. d	30. c
31. d									

Chapter 9

1. a	2. d	3. d	4. d	5. d	6. b	7. d	8. d	9. d	10. d
11. a	12. d	13. d	14. d	15. d	16. b	17. d	18. a	19. d	20. c
21. a	22. b	23. d	24. b	25. a	26. c	27. d	28. d	29. d	30. d
31. b	32. d	33. d	34. d	35. b	36. d	37. b	38. a	39. d	40. c
41. c	42. d	43. d	44. a	45. d	46. d	47. d	48. c	49. d	50. d
51. b	52. c	53. b	54. d	55. a	56. d	57. c	58. d	59. c	60. a
61. d	62. a	63. d	64. c	65. d	66. c	67. d	68. d	69. a	70. d
71. d									

www.ingramcontent.com/pod-product-compliance
Lightning Source LLC
Chambersburg PA
CBHW082052230426
43670CB00016B/2864